The Gospel according to Gamaliel

THE GOSPEL ACCORDING TO GAMALIEL

By

GERALD HEARD

WIPF & STOCK · Eugene, Oregon

Wipf and Stock Publishers
199 W 8th Ave, Suite 3
Eugene, OR 97401

The Gospel According to Gamaliel
By Heard, Gerald
ISBN 13: 978-1-60608-982-8
Publication date 10/01/2009

Previously published by Harper & Brothers, 1945

Photograph of Gerald Heard by Jay Michael Barrie

TO

CHRISTOPHER WOOD

Series Foreword

Gerald Heard (Oct. 6, 1889–Aug. 14, 1971) wrote nearly forty books during the course of a distinguished career. His Cambridge-trained, curiosity-ridden mind left no stone unturned in its intellectual investigations. His nonfiction topics ranged from history to philosophy, from psychology to religion, and virtually everything in between. These issues were woven together by a single unifying theme—the evolution of consciousness. During the 1940s, after he had relocated to America, after he had rediscovered his religious roots, and after he had begun a rigorous daily meditation practice, Gerald, as he was always known, mobilized his energies into establishing Trabuco College in Southern California. Trabuco was the first coeducational spiritual community in America to incorporate ecumenical, nonsectarian religious principles and practices. And practice the Trabuco attendees did, meditating three times daily in order to accelerate the spiritual evolution of their own individual consciousnesses.

Having previously published a dozen mostly academic and popular science books, Gerald turned his attention to religion during this war-torn decade. Gerald's religious writings from this period consist of eight key contributions that address practical and inspirational spiritual themes. Of these, four primary Heardian religious works are initially included in this vital new Wipf & Stock series, with more to follow. Collectively these books comprise Gerald's quintessential statements on the spiritual path, and a person could conceivably use these volumes as guidebooks for their entire spiritual journey.

And here is Gerald at his very best—preaching the evolution of consciousness and offering practical advice on how to attain it. Gerald's rotating roles as visionary historian, maverick cosmologist, and prescient philosopher are all present in the background of these religious works. But at the forefront is Gerald the practicing mystic and knowing docent, gushing forth an ebullient but sometimes cautionary narrative on traversing the spiritual path from start to finish. His accounts, as confirmed by classic mystics and traditional texts, derive from his own subjective experience. The ringing truth of his musings will cause the receptive reader first to reflect, then to act, propelled by the stirring contagion of Gerald's boundless enthusiasm.

In the 1940s, novelist Christopher Isherwood wrote that Gerald, "has influenced the thought of our time, directly and indirectly, to an extent which will hardly be appreciated for another fifty years." Those fifty years have now passed. Some of Gerald's ideas have fallen by the wayside, while others lie dormant still waiting to sprout. Yet a good many have blossomed into unspoken cornerstones of contemporary thought. The widespread establishment of religious communities has become commonplace. Religious syncretism, ecumenical studies, and interdisciplinary, eclectic approaches lie at the vanguard of progressive religious thought. Contemplative meditation practices have gained broad acceptance across a spectrum of diverse traditions. Theories on the evolution of consciousness abound. Colleges and whole movements of thought now regularly explore the transpersonal realm of pure consciousness.

But what makes Gerald's farsighted approach to religion especially relevant now is what made it relevant when these books were first published—he is espousing timeless truths. The reader is supplied with a map, compass, and numerous exhortations of attainment, as well as warnings of the pitfalls to avoid while embarking on this singlemost important sojourn in life. Gerald offered no quick fixes or shortcuts. He advocated a wholesale restructuring of one's entire being through, "the skilled, conscious training of our spirits." He advanced a holistic approach long before holistic approaches became popular.

Within these books is found Gerald's essential message: "Our whole life must become intentional and purposive, instead of a series of irrelevant events, adventures, and accidents. We must ourselves deliberately develop ourselves. That evolution which follows will show itself in a threefold development: in growth of conduct, of character and of consciousness itself. The world exists for man to achieve union with God. The meaning of all, the purpose and the end of all is one thing, seeing God."

When revisiting Gerald's spiritual classics in this new century, we are entering the very heart of religious experience. We are treading the path trodden by serious spiritual practitioners, be they novices or seasoned mystics. We are undertaking a journey of utmost significance, leading to pulsating union with God. As able guide and modern interpreter of mysticism, Gerald Heard nimbly and authoritatively beckons us toward the Goal that each of us was born to realize in this very life.

John Roger Barrie
Literary Executor of Gerald Heard
Nevada City, California
January 22, 2007

Thanks especially to Ted Lewis of Wipf and Stock Publishers, and Craig Tenney and Phyllis Westberg of Harold Ober Associates for their valuable assistance in bringing this series into print.

For more information on Gerald Heard, visit geraldheard.com, the Gerald Heard Official Website.

—JRB

Speaking for Gamaliel

by Rabbi Zalman Schachter-Shalomi

2009

There are some pivotal encounters in our lives, and for me one of these was meeting Gerald Heard. It isn't easy to estimate the impact of his person and thought when it has become so pervasive in the system files of my thought processor. My work in Spiritual Eldering that became expressed in my book *From Age-ing To Sage-ing* is based on Gerald's *The Five Ages of Man*, where he can be seen as the savant, the repository of the most encompassing cosmology of his generation. (What a pity that people in his day did not appreciate the scope of his contemplative mind and that of Teilhard de Chardin.) Much of what I have thought and written about concerning our spiritual process is influenced by his *Training For a Life of Growth*. In this work he served as the guru teaching the *Upaya*—the skillful means of inner work. I got much delight from his *Gabriel and the Creatures*. When reading him and listening to him with my inner ear, I felt like a wide-eyed child listening to the wise grandpa telling the story how it really happened.

But the book in which he astonished me to the core was his *The Gospel According to Gamaliel*. In view of the spate of Gospel material published lately it is meet and just that this book be made available again. Certainly the hidden Gnostic Gospels that were found in Nag Hamadi and the Gospel of Judas recently discovered and discussed brought about an interest on the part of some to understand not only the life of Jesus, but also what the Germans called the *Sitz-im-Leben*, the environment in which occurred what has been termed "the greatest story ever told."

A search for the original meaning of the message of the Good News has bearing on many current events in the United States and the world over. There is what is rearing up in the battle between Christianity and Islam, and of course there is also a battle between Islam and Judaism. Despite the advances of Vatican II, there are still many areas of stress between Judaism and Christianity.

Someone who had never heard of Christianity and the Gospels would be amazed at the difference between various Christians, specifically, between those whose ecumenically embracing emphasis is on the virtues of the Beatitudes, and those voices that come from a rigid, triumphalist reading of some of the texts of the Gospels, Acts of the Apostles, the disputational Epistles, and the visions of the rapture from the Apocalypse. On the one hand we have the compassionately embracing parts of the Sermon on the Mount and the descriptions of healing and consolation, and on the other hand is a zealous insistence on an unreasonable inerrancy of the Bible in the King James version (especially when it can be clearly demonstrated that the translators failed to understand the original meaning of the Hebrew, Aramaic, and Greek languages).

Similarly, we read portions of the Quran emphasizing Allah's compassion and clemency as well as the teachings of the virtues of kindness, and yet the daily reported atrocities also in the name of the Quran make us wonder what it is that brings about this polarization into two opposing attitudes.

The two camps claiming that they are the best readers of the sacred texts are arrayed against each other. There has been an increase in the surface tension between the two. On the one side is a cosmology that embraces all creation with compassion, and on the other side is a triumphalist attitude that "our religion and version of the truth is the only genuine one."

It need not be so. It takes the genius of Gerald Heard to get into the mind of Gamaliel, to demonstrate how even in the life of Jesus there occurred a turn from the all-accepting and embracing Savior, to the now polarized and attacked Jesus and the harshness that he at times expressed when cornered. As we follow Paul, especially in the Acts of the Apostles, we can see him swinging from the zealous attacker of Christianity to the zealous defender of his own idiosyncratic reading of what Jesus' message was about. Gerald Heard places himself in the mind of the wise and sage Gamaliel and gives us much understanding about how these polarizing tensions began, grew, and increased.

When Gerald Heard wrote *The Gospel According to Gamaliel*, he preceded the discovery of the Dead Sea Scrolls. The Qumran archives have given us an understanding of the conditions of that time, the divisions that occurred in Judaism, and the political vicissitudes of life under the Roman hegemony even before the Temple was destroyed. While at the same time that there were mystics and apocalyptic visionaries, there were also some who sought to find the kingdom of God in the desert. When we realize what Qumran was about we can make sense of the fact that the Christian Desert Fathers, monks and nuns, and subsequently the dervishes of Islam, all share in that holy separated way of life that the Qumran community lived.

There were some people who claimed that during the silent years of Jesus, that is to say the years between the time when he was with his parents in the Temple in Jerusalem and later on when he began his ministry, he must have been with those people in Qumran. I am also aware that there have been some people who claim that he had gone to India and learned there the secrets of yoga and of transformation from human into divine. However, this claim makes much less sense to me because there are no cultural traces of that, while there are cultural traces of Qumran in the proclamation of John the Baptizer and the expectation of a redeemer at that time.

What was missing for many of us was to have insight into the way in which the Jewish community dealt with the emerging church after the demise of Jesus, during the days of Paul. We are told that Rabban Shimon ben Gamaliel (the erstwhile teacher of Saul of Tarsus, later the Paul of the Epistles who became an apostle after his conversion on the road to Damascus,) was also of the house of David and had quite a legitimate case to claim Royal descent. He didn't do so, in the humble way of his ancestor Hillel. He continued to guide his people in matters of religion, and from all his halakhic decisions one can see that he was a very balanced person.

It isn't fair to diagnose a person like Saul of Tarsus as bipolar, epileptic, or paranoid from the distance of history. Nevertheless, in part of the traces he left us in his letters and utterances we can see the zeal that made him feel especially designated to pursue his evangelism. That evangelism was at first against the new Christian community, which was why he started out on the road to Damascus. One cannot help but be puzzled about his arguments that he offers in Koine Greek addressing them to the converted believers of the new communities, but still there is an awareness that in the back of his mind he is also speaking to the community of adherents to the new covenant who were of Jewish extraction. So much of this argument is trying to justify what he is doing to the members and elders of the church in Jerusalem.

Heard also had a sympathetic place for James, the leader of the new believers in Jerusalem. In the Acts of the Apostles it shows that the personalities of Shim'on Kepha (a.k.a. Peter the apostle) and Paul clashed from time to time. What Paul seems to want to justify in terms couched in halachic reasoning, Peter simply justifies as a result of direct visions that he received from his master about what is kosher and what is not.

And when we follow Paul in his leadership when he had acquired disciples, we can see in the Acts of the Apostles that he had some concern about where he would celebrate the feast of Passover. He sends off his gentile converts to Rome so that they would be traveling during Passover and not be able to keep as many rules and regulations connected with that feast. He and the Jewish disciples would remain in the place where they could observe the holiday and only later would travel on to meet the others in Rome.

Rabban Gamaliel inquires from Paul about the Man from Nazareth. The rabbi expresses great sympathy, and he is also aware that there is a lack of balance in the way in which Jesus completely wants to switch himself and his people into what he considered the kingdom of God. However he does this in a precipitous way that does not pay any attention to the larger picture and to the many sacrifices that would entail.[1]

Considering the martyrdom of Rabbi Akiba, whose skin was flayed while he was alive, and his nine colleagues and disciples who were put to death under torture at the hands of the Romans after the Destruction of the Temple and the Siege of Betar, the specific story of the Gospels becomes part of the weave of the history of that time.

1. Looking at Mel Gibson and his movie *The Passion of the Christ*, it seems that the Christian world is disproportionately focused on the individual story of Jesus' suffering, which was so graphically and unfairly portrayed the way in which Gibson depicted it. (However, I really was impressed by the Aramaic that was spoken in the movie. He must have gotten quite a bit of help to train his actors to speak the lines. While he went for Latin in order to stay close to his father's commitment to the Church before *Aggiornamento*, he apparently forgot that the original language of the Gospels was Greek and that the people in the holy land at that time had several languages as their *lingua franca*—Aramaic, Greek, along with the official Latin in which Pontius Pilate communicated with his superiors and other officials.)

Gerald Heard widens our perspective to see the larger landscape of those turbulent days during which the drama of the life and death of Jesus and the apostleships of Paul and Peter took place. With deep intuition he finishes the book with Peter's pontificate.

I am curious to this day how Gerald heard knew so much of the background of Gamaliel. (Could I possibly claim that he channeled Gamaliel? I wouldn't be surprised if Gerald Heard had those shamanic sensitivities.)

So enter the mind of Gerald Heard and see through his eyes looking through the eyes of Gamaliel the story that was pivotal in the history of humanity. In his preface he shares his motivation for writing this small/huge book. You will find that he expresses many inklings you have had before.

• • •

Rabbi Zalman Schachter-Shalomi is founder of the Jewish Renewal and Spiritual Eldering movements, a pioneer in ecumenical relations, and a participant in worldwide interfaith dialogue. He has taught at the University of Manitoba, Temple University, and Naropa University. Reb Zalman, as he is widely known, has been an influential spiritual teacher for four decades. He has written or co-written several groundbreaking books, including *From Age-ing to Sage-ing: A Profound New Vision of Growing Older*, and *Jewish With Feeling: A Guide to Meaningful Jewish Practice.*

Introduction

GAMALIEL is known to history. The facts are brief but they are all of cardinal significance. His time, his place, his character combine to give him a unique interest. His grandfather was the great Hillel, who not only became president of the Sanhedrin, but who also by his deep learning, piety, humility and passionate love of peace, brought the thought of Judaism into that form which has made it able to survive as a lofty ethic until the present. The nationalist movement under the Maccabees had failed. An earthly kingdom of righteousness had been tried and had miscarried. The Temple with its blood sacrifices was becoming increasingly a spiritual anachronism. Most of the Chosen People no longer resided in the Promised Land. The synagogue was becoming their real religious center and their real worship the reading of the Law and the practice of prayer, not the sacrifices and the rituals at the altars. Hillel made the beginning of this process clear. Gamaliel, his grandson, carried on the development. His eminence was recognized also; he was president of the Sanhedrin and the first Jewish teacher to carry as a definite honorific title the term "Rabban." In turn his grandson, Gamaliel the Second, who also rose to be the Sanhedrin's president, brought the process to completion. When in his time the Temple was destroyed, that destruction was the cutting of an umbilical cord. Judaism henceforth was a religion free from local adhesions to the site of its birth.

So Gamaliel the First was the keystone of that span of

five generations during which Judaism found a positive answer to the two most searching questions that can be addressed to a religion: Firstly, "Could it live without a political aspect, a 'Regnum'?" Secondly, Could it live without a priestly center and frame, a 'Sacerdotum'?" Of him may be said that he was the chief link in that chain which made Judaism a world religion.

This were enough for one man's fame. But, set at the center of these five generations, are three other generations whose apparent influence on mankind was greater even than that of Judaism itself. Hillel, as a spiritual father, had, like Abraham, two children. The "Isaac"—the one "born in the family"—was the Chassidic-Pharisee school of the synagogues, the leaders of which were Hillel's own bodily descendants. The "Ishmael"—the one "born outside of the family"—is harder to trace. We have, however, clear if broken evidence of its initial stage in the Essene and Nazarite movement culminating in John the Baptist. This is the forerunner phase, the period of waiting, questioning, looking forward, seeking, defining the form and function of what should be revealed. Then this, too, enters its keystone phase. With the historic Jesus comes the poetic prophet who fulfills this expectation. He is spiritually of Hillel's school. Seventy-five per cent of his sayings have been found in the utterances of that school. The favorite maxim of Hillel's group was the Golden Rule. His teaching, stressing humility, love, patience, that the meek inherit the earth, that gentle righteousness and unwearied forgiveness is the one sacrifice for sin that God requires, that man is forgiven and sanctified by that relationship alone, that all mankind is God's child and men are all brethren—all this is Hillelism delivered with the magic of a poet, the power of a healer, and the drama of an identifying personality.

Further, this Joshua bar Joseph of Galilee was the contemporary of Gamaliel, grandson of Hillel. Gamaliel was probably ten years old when Joshua was born. Both quite possibly, were of Davidic descent—certainly Hillel's house claimed it. As the Sanhedrin did not permit full membership until a man was forty, Gamaliel would therefore most probably have been elected immediately after Joshua's death.

The first generation of forerunners (Essene, Nazarite, John the Baptist) had passed into the second, the keystone generation, when these rays converge into the focus of a single life, and a voice answering "I am he." Now, in turn, the second generation passes into the third, the generation of stylization, when the particular historical figure is crystallized into a universal symbol, the Christ. An avatar takes three generations to incarnate. We can see this growth in the Gospels from Mark to John and the development in the Pauline Epistles from the personal Saviour of his first letters—"The Man from Heaven"—to the Creator of the universe of Paul's last speculative writings. Mark and Paul the convert, who had been but lately Saul, have different needs to be met and to meet. Paul, the master of "the Mysteries," selling his new syncretic faith broadcast among the Gentiles, contemptuous of the Law, no longer interested in Judaism save as a foe that must capitulate unconditionally, this Paul and that even stranger author of the Fourth Gospel are at one: the historic Jesus is simply a place of departure for cosmological speculations and theories.

The vast crystallized structure which finally grows and precipitates into the complex called Christendom has, then, as the base of its pattern two original faces: a story told by a Galilean spectator called Simon, the fisherman, and a convulsive experience befallen a bitter critic of that story, a speculative but violent thinker called Saul of Tarsus. Gamaliel stands at the source of both these men's active lives. It is he who gives the first judicial hearing, judgment, and toleration to that story which Simon, who appears before him, is going out to tell the world, a story which, when Simon has repeated it until it has become a polemical message, will finally, in Rome, be put into writing by Mark. It is Gamaliel also who gives the speculative and mystical interpretations of the Law, which makes the Law not a dead code but a way of life and light and love. Such a Law is, unlike the law of the Letter, beyond man's power. For the law of the spirit can never be kept in its fullness. This is Hillel's teaching. It declares that the Love of God makes the loving heart realize that it can never live up to the lawful demands of that Love. Therefore, he who loves God will always confess his own incapacity to fulfill the spiritual law. At the same time this teaching emphasizes the complementary truth—God's willingness to fulfill the Law in the hearts of all who open themselves to Him by love. It is this doctrine that Gamaliel taught his pupil Saul. But this divine paradox Saul's legalistic mind and twisted heart could not sustain. He broke the single antinomy of the divine truth into two and so sinned against Hebraism's great achievement, the unity of God.

Gamaliel is, then, not only the keystone in the history of Judaism when it had to span the gap between a sacrificial and spiritual religion, but he points to a possible line of departure for the whole religion of Western man. In his central years and under his eyes the decision was taken whether to develop the doctrine of a purely spiritual religion or fall back on the cruder earlier notion of substitutional sacrifice; whether to hold God's mercy and justice in a fertile antinomy or to separate Saviour and Creator, Redeemer and Ultimate Judge. The history of Christianity is largely, therefore, an oscillation between the idea of a God who is an unappeasable Law and a Saviour who delivers his followers from any responsibility to Law. Perhaps today Hillel's doctrine comes closest to that of the spiritually minded, closest to that Eternal Gospel, that Perennial Philosophy which is now recognized as the living nerve at the center of every great religion, the common creative principle in all the creeds which have produced saints. Certainly today our critical historical knowledge has brought us to Gamaliel's position. Had he written a gospel, it must have been in its main facts very close to that picture which textural research and anthropological insight now perceive behind the polemical accounts which the early Church gave of its origins. This narrative sketch is, then, an attempt to see what the dawn of Christianity looked like through the eyes of one who was of great scholarship, of great tolerance, of great loyalty to the Law, and of great love for mankind.

Such an attempt might well be temerarious if the intention were to suggest that the design so deduced is the one possible profile that can be obtained from an honest and informed study of the Synoptists. The Higher Criticism, which has given the elements for the character of Joshua in the following narrative, may pass into a criticism still higher, because possessed of a deeper insight into the supreme problems of spirituality. But the attempt to range these findings in narrative form may help toward seeing where actually those problems lie. When we realize that authorities of the greatest scholarship can honestly and completely differ as to the recorded teaching of the historic Jesus on such supremely important issues as marriage, war and eternal punishment, we can understand the statement that of all the great religions Christianity is most capable of ambiguous teaching and ambiguous results in morals, methods and cosmology.

There is another pressing and topical reason why one brought up as a Christian should attempt to view through the eyes of a Hebrew that channel through which the Eternal Gospel has come to Western man. The differences and tensions between Gentiles and Jews have not lessened in the last two thousand years. Today they are not merely one of the disgraces of our common culture; they are not the least of its perils. One of the causes of that conflict is the different construction put by Christian and Jew on the life of Joshua bar Joseph of Nazareth. Anything which will help Gentiles to understand how much their Christ owed to the Judaism of his day; anything which will help Jews to regard Joshua as great with all the greatness of their beloved prophets, may do something, however slight, to help rid our civilization of one of its worst blots. And, should such a mutual understanding be achieved, it might well do more for the world's peace than any number of pacts. Hebrew and Gentile scholarship have jointly done much to demonstrate this important case. The ordinary world—Gentile and Jew—seems, however, still unaware of it. A duty lies, therefore, on any writer to attempt, in whatever manner he may, to popularize this "peaceful good news to all men of good will." Thus some small contribution may be made toward the spread of that charity, which was never taught with greater beauty than by the last of the Hebrew prophets whose voice has spoken to more hearts than any of his inspired race.

The Gospel according to Gamaliel

Chapter I

"I *WAS* young and am now old," the Psalmist's words are now mine. The threescore years and ten, which he gives as man's term, I have accomplished. For a generation—since my fortieth year—I have served Israel, as judge, as administrator, as interpreter of the Holy Law. I have made THE SEVEN RULES OF INTERPRETATION framed by my holy grandfather Hillel to be accepted by all. In this my time and for me has the title "Rabban," used till now as a courtesy address, become a title of precedence. This year, at my request, I shall be granted to lay down the highest ministry of the Holy People, as Nasi, Prince President of the Sanhedrin.

Can I, on looking back, say, as says the Psalmist, I have seen God's justice manifested in this life: I have never seen the righteous unjustified or their seed begging their bread? Can I say, looking forward, as is said in the chronicles of the just, I have seen my children's children and peace upon Israel? These are questions which any man looking back over his life must ask. For me in these days they have a double urgency. My grandfather, the holy Hillel, was by the grace of the Most High, permitted to see in me, his son's son, not merely a grandson after the flesh, but his loving and reverent son of the spirit. My grandfather, loving above all the peace of God, was permitted by an inspired wisdom so to interpret the Holy Scriptures that he wrought a peaceful rebirth in Israel, bringing out of the ancient treasury jewels of recovered wisdom and making much that had become tarnished a fresh splendor before God and a new light for man. He indeed saw a new peace opening before Israel so that beside the ancient, honored, inflexible rite and ritual centered in the Holy Temple, a new contemporary spirituality might spread far and wide through synagogues wherever the righteous would meet to hear the Law and the prophets and to pray. Thus all mankind should see the light among them and be blessed. My lifelong duty and love has been to propagate his teaching and favor its practice. I am unworthy to be his child and his successor. But I have cherished in my heart this encouragement: that, as I grew, he chose personally to teach me, and when he died he called me from among our kindred, standing in prayer beside his bed and, bidding me kneel, he laid his hands on my head, granting me the spiritual birthright, calling on me the blessing given by Elijah to Elisha and charging me to complete his ministry.

And now I am old and God has granted to me also to see my grandson grown, and I, too, can have no doubt that here is my stock standing strong before the God of Israel and, greater blessing, here is the mind of my grandfather, the mind that has striven to express itself in me, once more manifested in our line. My grandson, Gamaliel, all see as a judge and ruler who shall fulfill my grandfather's teaching and confirm and give form to my initial applications of that teaching.

But do I see, stretching before him, peace upon Israel? Has my grandfather's hope and initial achievement been fulfilled? Have Temple and synagogue, the ancient sacrificial system and the ever-self-renewing Law of Living Mercy gone on in growing reciprocant richness side by side? I cannot say so. I had thought to see this the way of the Lord. The path as it has been disclosed is darker, yet it may be His way. I had thought my grandfather had been sent to show us how to pass through the waves of destruction, hemming around the Holy People and Place. Rather than a new Moses leading through the Red Sea, he was perhaps a Noah, building an Ark in which a small remnant might survive, floating over a submerged world. Certainly the hope that our nation, as a nation with the Holy City, its Holy Temple, priesthood, sacrifices, and shrine, can survive, grows dim in my heart. A darkness lies over the land. Not a season goes by but men of violence, that violence my grandfather opposed utterly as the most terrible of the temptings of God, commit fresh violence. There can be no doubt, the Zealots are now organized to provoke revolt. They strike at the Romans to make them strike back; at the Herodians to make these temporizers take sides for once and all; at the High Priest's household and the great officials to terrorize the administration to break with imperial compromise. The end is near and can be foreseen. Jerusalem, which has rejected the prophets and the growing interpretation of the Law of Merciful Righteousness, will, as before, bring down upon it vengeance. For, as it is written as the Book of Chronicles closes the Canon, "There is no remedy."

Yet assuredly, as assuredly as the Ark rode out the deluge, will the invisible Ark of the Spiritual Covenant outride this inundation. Though the tides of violence and of time engulf the Temple and its altars, leaving not one stone upon another, the Eternal Law shall remain and the People shall serve It and be preserved by It.

Therefore did I, too, prepare the building of such an Ark and lay ready for this my grandson's successor those materials whereby he may frame it. Hence I have written this story. Why do I think that the deluge is nigh? Not because the outward foes of Israel are menacing. The Persian and the Greek ruled us. They have passed and we remain. Rome will pass also and the Holy People remain. A nation may never be destroyed by arms, for arms cannot touch the soul which creates and sustains the outer form. But the People today are sundered in their soul, divided in heart. Their vitality is therefore halved and their kingdom must therefore be divided. When the life of the body has ebbed, then mortification begins in the lower members, and the life of the trunk can often only be saved by cutting off the limb which, once an expression of man's strength, has now become a bridgehead of death. So today Israel may have to make such a choice. Has the People the vitality to sustain the full structure of a Holy Nation—a theocracy, an ancient sacerdotal system, a hereditary hierarchy, a country, a capital, a Temple, and, beside this, a spiritual heredity, a living tradition spreading outwards over the world and adapting to world needs? My grandfather prepared for such a sublime destiny—an Israel developing both its own life and also leading the spiritual life of all the peoples. I write this record, for it is the record of the miscarriage of that great hope, that we might fulfill all God's promise to the patriarchs and so out of Abraham should all the nations be blessed. I write it so that my grandson may be guided how to act in this narrower choice, the salvage of the Holy People when their outward forms and their opportunity of leading mankind have both passed from them.

I believe, with resigned sorrow before the just judgment of the Most High, that we knew not the day of our visitation. I believe that what I shall leave on record will prove that God sent us a unique opportunity and we shrank from it, as from an intrusion. I am convinced that when my grandfather as forerunner had proclaimed the oncoming of THE DAY OF THE LORD and shown what was required of us to welcome that day and to enter upon it, we failed to understand. I blame no man or group of men. Were we not all one People, bound together in truth and charity to serve with one mind and one heart God's will? We are all to blame: priests and prophets, scribes and Levites; Sadducee and Nazarite; Pharisee and Herodian; those who came eating and drinking and those who fasted in the wilderness; the impatient Zealot and the stubborn Meek; the compromised Administrator and the scornful Simplifier who could only criticize, denounce and defy.

Here only would I set down the history of what I saw, lived through and acted in—the tale of those fatal and crucial years in which the moment of opportunity brimmed at our feet and we failed to take it. This great crisis began, as I have said, with the wonderful promise of my grandfather's ministry. I foretell it will not close until my grandson has shown what, out of the failure of that hope, may be salvaged. This I know, that in my lifetime it passed us by. We saw the great gate of world-wide opportunity swing open and shut. Now remains only the postern through which the remnant may escape. Before these eyes, which soon must darken on this wavering scene—to open under the Eternal Light—there has been performed that supreme tragedy of misunderstanding, that tragedy whereby those who were sent to contribute each to the other's fulfillment, so that from the mutual kindling of their hearts and minds there should have sprung the light to lighten the Gentiles and to be the glory of the People of Israel, no light sprang but only eclipse and darkness. Let this be read by my son of my name, child of my loins and heart and mind. Let him read and judge. And any that shall read after him, let them read and understand, condemning none of us lest they themselves be condemned, but learning from us not to miss their day of opportunity when God shall send it.

Chapter II

THIS WORK has caused in myself much heart-searching. I must own that in this event I am not unprejudiced. When a teacher has lost his best pupil to another teacher, the first teacher is perhaps not the best judge of the second. When that pupil, always headstrong, violent and impatient of authority, rejects his first trainer, not in favor of the second, but in favor of a theory which he has constructed about this second, his original master may call this not a change of authority, but the setting up of the self, disguised as another. When the pupil's teaching reproduces hardly a word of his master's instruction, but is an elaborate interpretation of what he maintains is the significance of his master's death, then it needs a very guarded pen not to write down such teaching as not of the Law nor of the prophets nor the Wisdom, but a hybrid myth framed to entice the Gentiles and to divide the Jews. No more will I say than this; so that he who reads may know what this tragedy has cost him who describes it, and may approve my witness that before the Eternal I tell the truth as I saw it and bear ill will to none.

It is not true to say that we of the Temple and the Law were one and all rooted in the past. There were many of us who as the days darkened looked for a light, believing in the words of the prophet that "as dusk falls then shall the light return." My own teacher of my later years of pupilhood was such a man. He was a seeker and often had said to me, "If Issachar, 'the ass bending beneath two burdens,' nevertheless was the mount on which was reared the last Deliverer, the Maccabean Judas, shall we then say that deliverance shall not again come from the outskirts?" He spoke, too, of a Galilean boy that once had stayed on after a Passover, asking such questions as to the eternal promises of deliverance that the child's earnestness remained in his heart many days. He had asked the boy whether he would not come and live in his household and, since his house served the Temple, so enter on the Father's service. The child's parents, however, would not hear of such adoption, as nearly always happens.

Therefore, when I heard that prophets were again arising, I said in my heart and to my fellow teachers, "Let us not refuse to learn because we teach and let us not shorten the arm of the Lord that He should not raise Him up witnesses in the outer courts." And when they said, "But unless these witnesses follow after us they will mislead the People," I answered, "If they be not of God He will not sustain them and they will fade away: while if they are from Him and we oppose them it is we who shall be found fighting against the Most High."

When, then, one of our own Levites had a son who became a Nazarite and as a desert dweller called all men to repentance, though his words were bitter and he railed against our party of strict observance, nevertheless I went with some of my fellows to hear him preach. He denounced us for coming to him because, he said, we had not repented and were not trusting in the spirit but in our pride of descent from Abraham. He had the power that the rigid have over the consciences of the lax, but, having not charity, he could not see among those who came to him some who were truly seeking the Lord.

It was therefore with joy that I heard of the coming of another prophet though in Galilee of the Gentiles. Again some of the strictest of the scribes, of the school of Shammai, warned me saying, "Search the Scriptures that you be not misled. Search and see, for out of Galilee arises no prophet." But I answered that our holy father Hillel had shown from the Scriptures that the Eternal is the Father of all. Therefore would He speak through any who would keep His Holy Law of love and righteousness. Did we not know that the flock of the Holy People were now scattered far beyond the fold of the Holy Land? From my grandfather I had also cherished the faith that wherever the Law was read in the simplest synagogue and pure prayer offered, there, as the Psalmist says, the lifting up of hands washed in innocency is an evening and a morning sacrifice. Because of this when I became a master in Israel I hastened to the aid of these sheep. I helped these who had no Holy Place in which to keep the Holy Tides by giving them an ordered Calendar; and to preserve the basis of the nation, the family, I gave them rulings as to the mutual rights of marriage. These laws I made and published with special letters for those in Galilee as well as to all of the Dispersion. They are witness that I was resolved my master's teaching should be illustrated in action. It may be, too, my concern for Galilee dates from that day when I went to find the prophet who had no prestige but his message, and was said to have no rule but the spirit of the Lord, which we hold is Love. For those who told me of him said that in his words love and light shone out. Always I had cherished the hope that we should know the true prophet in that he would fulfill the great prophecy of that fount of the prophets, Hosea. "I will have mercy and not sacrifice." In this hope I had remained a loyal member of the Pharisees of strict observance because, though some were Formalists, nevertheless in their avoidance of stress on sacrifice and in their exaltation of the deliverance of the Law of Righteousness and Mercy I saw the hope of Israel. Being assured, then, that this was the spirit of a new prophet's message I resolved that I would myself leave Jerusalem for a sojourn and see and hear if indeed this should be he for whom we looked.

The Passover was early that year. As soon as it was ended I set out north with but two attendants. The spring had gone only a few days in front of us, making the desolate places to rejoice. As we entered Galilee of the Gentiles, I thought that the Father who so garnished the dwelling places of the alien surely must care not less for them than He did for us who hived around our Holy Rock where the smell of incense and sacrificial blood is heavy.

We had little difficulty in finding where the new prophet was teaching. Indeed, as soon as we entered the lake region, everyone seemed to be talking about him. "God has remembered His People." "He has come, as is written, healing the sick, giving sight to the blind and casting out demons." So he is a thaumaturge, I said to myself. And, so hard is it for the seeker to shake off his worldly station, the teacher and administrator in me reflected with experienced relief: then he will not be attempting armed revolt. For he who heals can hardly regress to the baser appeal of violence. Even when other answerers to our inquiry called back, no doubt because they saw my white mule and phylacteries, "He, as do the true prophets, denounces the fat practitioners of religion," I held my peace and kept my judgment. Maybe the denunciations were not his, but what his borderland audience wished to hear and so would put into his mouth. What was the good of my coming, if on finding him, I only found myself already prejudiced?

Finally, when we were passing along the lakeside track a fisherman told us that the prophet had been preaching thereabouts.

"Only yesterday," he said, "the crowd was so great that he stepped into this boat of mine and spoke to them from the water just here. A wonderful man. They crowd on him as birds on corn seed. But he's always ready for them. Think of it: there was I watching the crowd edge down on the shore as I sculled my boat in. We had had a good catch the night before and I had left the yawl and the nets in the other cove where the jetty is. My younger brother was doing the selling with fishmongers. I wanted to slip up and see my wife's mother. She'd been sick with one of those spring fevers—they're hard on an old body. I couldn't make out first what the crowd was doing. Then as the boat slipped in closer I saw. They were crowding to hear a man who stepped backward as they pressed on him. They'd have crushed him otherwise, but he never stopped speaking, nor they advancing. He'll fall backwards into the water, I thought. And then (it was as neat and as natural as wind fills an unfurled sail) just as they had him hemmed, my boat's prow ran alongside the wet stone he was stepping onto. 'Do you think,' he asked them, 'you'd not put every penny into buying the field up there if you thought it had buried treasure?' And with that, as though he knew I'd come to offer him a chair, he stepped backward, seating himself in the thwarts and looked around on them for an answer. They simply gaped for more, and off he went with stories about merchants who gamble all they have on the giant pearls that come from the great seas and only a Herod can buy. They waded in to catch his words and, those at the back forcing the front ones deeper, some were almost up to their waists in the water."

"Suddenly he stopped, stood up in the prow and cried, 'If you've got ears you'll catch what I'm saying.' At that they looked at each other, puzzled. And while you could hear the whisper, 'What's he mean?' running like a breeze through lakeside reeds, he waved to me to scull again. The boat, which had begun to drift out, once more swung in and bumped the beach. He stepped ashore, the crowd gave, I pulled the dinghy up the shingle and he called at me over his shoulder, 'Come along.' I trotted off after him, the crowd only turning their heads to watch us. I thought he wanted something, but when I came up with him he said, as if we had known each other for years though I had never set eyes on him before, 'Why go on catching fish when men are waiting to be landed?' I said something about the two being different knacks. 'I'll teach you,' he said. 'I've got to get home just now. Got sickness in the house,' I replied, since I felt I ought to say where I was going. He simply strode along, going on talking about how men wanted life but couldn't get it unless they were saved. 'They're no fish, though they behave as though they were. They need to be saved.'

"He held me as he'd held the crowd and, before I knew it, we were at the house. He'd go off then, I was sure. But talking just the same, in he came with me. I could see, soon as I'd entered, the poor old lady was worse—a fever is a flame, it burns up a body. My wife came forward to say something but she stopped, the way I had stopped. For the man went straight up to the built-in bed, bent down, and the next thing we knew there the old mother stood holding onto his hand. 'I'm well, glory be! I never felt better,' she said, looking around at us with a kind of surprised, startled laugh. . . . 'Then perhaps you and your daughter will give Simon and me a little lunch?' he said smiling down at her. Off they bustled clacking like hens that have laid a couple of eggs. He left after thanking us."

The man paused. He seemed embarrassed at such a flow of narrative. But though his story was simple enough, his conviction overcame him.

"Do you know where he went?" I asked.

"I expect he'll be back again hereabouts. He's been preaching most days."

In the manner of fishermen his long-sighted eyes had been scanning the lake and the mountainside. As he stopped speaking, he gazed intently at a slope about half a mile away. "Bless me! That's he there now going up yonder slope and it looks as though he had a bigger crowd than yesterday even. You'll catch up with him if you take this shepherd's track around the head of the next valley."

I thanked him and we pushed along. He was right. The trail led around on the level, so we intercepted the swarm of people as they breasted the slope. Ahead of them strode a man with an easy swinging gait. I dismounted and, telling my men to hold my mule and stay with it and the baggage mule we had with us, I joined the crowd. We didn't have to climb much farther, for finding a big jutting boulder standing out like a corner crest of a building, he sat on that and without any preliminaries began to talk to them. They didn't need any catching or summoning: my fisherman was right about that. They were so silent that in the pauses I could hear the wavelets far down on the beach and my mules as they shuddered their flanks to drive off the early flies. This time he wasn't telling them stories. He looked around him, at us, and then at the grass slope, and at the sky.

"You all worry," he said, "it eats up your lives." And not only did one feel the truth of what he said, the fact that one was knotted up with worry, with cares, with anxieties for oneself, one's family, one's nation: one felt that he cared that we were careworn.

"Why do you worry?" He was asking it of each one of us, of me. "You believe in God, our Father?" I realized that I must ask myself that question with the utmost honesty.

Could I really say that I believed in that sense? "He cares for you, doesn't He?" We were now all looking at one another in a bewildered way, like sheep, before the gate, each waiting for the other. What he was saying was eternally commonplace, but the way he was saying it made the universal instant. I don't think the peasants around noticed that I was outwardly different. I know I knew that inwardly we were all equal, all children at a loss.

"Look!" he called to us, pointing to a cluster of spring anemones. The newly opened blossoms seemed to dye the ground with crimson and purple. So vivid was his gesture, you could have thought the petals had spread open at his beckoning. "Had the damasks of Solomon as fine a gloss and bloom as these petals? The Tyrian dyes could never imitate that glow. And tonight a rain squall will pelt them into the mud: while new petals, as fresh as ever will have unfolded." I felt that I had never seen spring flowers before. The life in them suddenly glowed out, not as something frail and evanescent but eternally strong. The blossoms themselves one saw as flames fluttering out from an unseen inextinguishable furnace of Being. A flock of small birds came up on the lake breeze and began to flutter above the early grasses, darting at seedheads which already were beginning to form. "The birds don't spend their time anxiously gathering stores into granaries. They take what the Father gives. If you'd be less anxious, you'd find more provision. You're always feeling you must count every penny. Why, your hairs are counted. Not a sparrow falls but the Father knows of it."

By then I'd come close as had all of the others, under the pressure of his call. "But Rabbi," I said, "birds do die in a hard winter." He swung around on me. His were certainly uncommon eyes. I felt it would be hard to give look for look, had they been shot with anger. But on the contrary, now they were lit with humor.

"Yes, and men go bald." We all laughed, for from my own temples the hair had begun to retreat. "What does all your worry serve? You can't by anxious thought make one hair grow, or keep it from falling or growing white, let alone persuade that closest possession that you have, your body, to grow even a few inches more once it has achieved its allotted stature." And then with a sudden tenderness he added, "He's equally kind to all His creatures. Rain and sunlight, He sheds them upon good and bad that they may be free to grow. He is the Giver. It is for us to use his gifts with the same openness. We should take and give and go, not clinging to what we call goods or possessions. We shouldn't shink from what we call the bad, from death and loss. We should take in and give out just as we take in His air. It is limitless—always ready to be taken in and given away. We should be utterly stintless as He is. The birds live lightly today, this moment, in the eternal now, because they are careless of the fact that they may be caught tomorrow and sold for a farthing. You've just got to learn to live, and to learn to live is to learn to give. That's the secret of all getting and any holding. Look at the grass; because it gives it comes back. Look at it now, bowing lightly to the wind. It's easy and flowing as we stiff anxious men can't be, though tomorrow it may be turning to brittle ash in the fire. Because it grows, and yields its seeds carelessly to the wind, and to the birds, after the hillside has been ablaze, on the very next rains, here it is as fresh as ever. It's the same with the trees; their life too, their growth too, depends exactly on those two things: 'Give,' or the storm will smash you and 'yield,' or your stock will fail.

"Why, you know it yourself in your work. Which of you

fishermen will go out in a boat that wouldn't give—you'd be swamped and sunk at the first squall. Indeed, you can't make use of a decent wind unless your mast has give, as well as your sails and tackle. They'd all be snapped to shreds if they weren't supple. Your nets, too, you'd lose your best catches, every fisherman, if the webbing had no give. The netting would tear and you'd lose netting and fish. You farmers see the same thing. If you haven't new wineskins with plenty of give in them, the new vintage will burst them and be lost before you've had a drop to drink. The land itself has to be given to, before it can give. Try to get before you've given and you'll starve. Bread can't come to you unless you'll give away back into the soil the best of the wheat. You don't need anyone to teach you that. Every sowing time don't you throw the seed willingly into the flooded meadows? What a fool you look to the fool that doesn't know! You've lost your wheat now for good, he's sure. But you're the knowing one. You wait for months and then there'll be a harvest giving you back a hundredfold. The same law runs through everything. You must start by giving. You can only get what you give. Give a hard fist and you get it back; give an open hand and an open hand will clasp yours. Give a generous gift, just for the joy of giving, and you will see, men will shame you by pressing back on you far more than ever you gave them.

"But you are asking, how does one get the power to give? Why, from the giver of all, Himself, from Him who gave you your life, your mind, your everything. You're all pretty tough now and you're perhaps a bit proud that you're nobody's fool. You've all dealt some hard deals and mean blows. You know you have. But that's not the whole story, is it? That's one side: there's another. The tough side falls off when you get home. Your small son runs to you

'Give me a cake.' Are you hard with *him*? Do you try to save for yourself by giving him a stone that might look like a cake? You're coming up with the catch and your eldest runs out asking you to give him one of the fish; do you try to trick him by giving him a snake instead? If you were a shrewd businessman you ought to be consistent. Why do you give your best when you're asked? Why, because you want to see your son happy. Well, if you are twisted, and yet untwist because your son trusts you, can you doubt? Won't the Father, who is Goodness itself, who is always, first and last, from start to finish, the Giver? Won't he give you His best if you ask Him? And what is His best? Why, His very nature, His creative power, His divine power to give and go on giving, forgiving and creating forever. Ask Him. He can't refuse, far less than you can. You're His child. And how He gives! Try and see. Seek, you'll find. Ask, He'll give. Trust Him, He'll surely grant. He is the same with you as He is with every living thing that He has made. The fault is you won't live now. You're always frightened to, because of what you think will happen later. Leave that to Him, take what he gives you today."

But my words, as I repeat his sayings, are as dead as dead grass or a dead bird. It was his saying them that gave them life, his incomparable aptness, as though the idea, the word, the incident he pointed to, were all come together in a chord. He wasn't teaching morality, and choosing words, and hunting for illustrations, as we scribes so often do. The man, his voice, the spring scene, were all one. There was a lovely inevitability, a wholeness about it. Indeed, even we listeners became part, were merged in it. The sunlight on the lake, the wind moving up the grass shoulders of the hill, the birds, flowers, the peasants, the rather weary, prematurely earnest religious ruler—we were all fused in the mild flame of his beauty. I looked from him to the crowd and I could see with my own sight they were weather-battered, work-bitten laborers. But for a moment they were alight in his light. For a moment, as we heard the breeze as music and saw the daylight as the Shekinah, we did love each other as ourselves; we were one.

But already he had risen and I saw the sun was overhead. He must have been speaking quite a while, though he seemed only to have said half a dozen sentences. He was striding away up the hill towards its crest. None of us followed now. He seemed to have the power both to draw men when he spoke and, when he ceased, to be able to break the current and to dismiss them, as a king terminates an audience by withdrawing into the inner palace.

For a moment I hesitated whether to follow him, but obeyed my feeling to respect his solitude. He certainly gave himself liberally and when he would withdraw he should not be hindered. The comments of the dispersing crowd were also worth attention. "Galilee's got a prophet at last." "The priests won't like it, will they!" "Nor the Pharisees." "He doesn't mind standing up to them." "Oh, I think sometimes he goes too far. You know what happened at his own village up at Nazareth's synagogue." "Well, all I know when he talks I could listen until dark." "Ah, when he speaks what he knows about God, for a moment we all seem to know."

The crowd had dispersed into chattering groups by the time I had rejoined my small party. I told them, as there would be plenty of daylight in which to cover the distance, we could push on to Nazareth. The road was good and we arrived there in the midafternoon. I told my men to arrange for us at the caravanserai, to have a meal ready at sundown. I myself strolled into the village. It was a typical little hill town, set well on a steep bluff with good enough houses occupied by sturdy folk. Good water and good earth make good men; I have had enough to do with books to know that character more often springs from earth and water than from words. Have I not said in my teaching that they who know may be of several types? The scholar with his rolls travels not the only road to knowledge. He who possesses skill with his hands, he also is a child, taught of our common mother, the Holy Wisdom. These countryside craftsmen were some of them already coming in from the fields and looked at me with neither challenge nor servility. Strangers up there, where whole nations mingle, awake neither suspicion nor wonder. A knot of people were gathered around the fountain. I asked the way to the synagogue. They nodded, a little further up the street. As I came to the very modest building an old scribe was coming out. I greeted him in the name of the Lord and he paused, looking at me carefully. When he had returned my greeting with good old-fashioned precision, he asked, after a moment's hesitation,

"Surely from Jerusalem?"

"Yes."

"And a loving student of the Law!"

"I hope so."

"I go into the place of prayer here every day to read the Holy Promises and to pray that they may come before long to fulfillment. May I for a few moments speak with you, sir? The prophet Malachi, as the Canon closes, promises that if God lovers will but meet and speak of their hope the day may come closer." He was a touching old man; a type of village scribe I have often found in country places; cherishing the Law and looking for its further realization.

We sat down together in the late afternoon light on the stone at the west door. After a few moments of silence I decided to lead up to my personal question. "How, Rabbi, do you think the signs of the times should be read? How may we train our hearing to catch the first footfalls of Him who is to come?"

"Your question is my own," he replied. "I'm always asking myself that very thing and searching Scripture so as to be ready. The prophet Daniel says much of a great appearing. Another Scripture only tells us that he will suddenly come to His Temple. Surely it must be at Jerusalem?" I nodded, though I caught some doubt in the question.

"Surely?" he questioned again.

So I added, "Have you any doubt?"

"No," he said tremulously, "no, but perhaps a hope." And then turning to me with sudden disarming confidence, "I have no one to tell. You love the Lord. May I not trust you on that?"

I was moved and turning to him touched his frontal and mine with my two hands: "As we are the Eternal's and serve His Law let us share the hope that we have in His Promises."

"You are learned in the Law. Could the Lord's Messenger come from the outskirts and come to Jerusalem?"

"You mean . . . ?"

"I began to have a hope, but now I am further bewildered."

"Father, tell me this story and then I will give you my judgment."

"We in Galilee are, I know, outsiders. But that we are despised makes some of us more devout. We have had some righteous men, though unlearned, in this very village. One of the best was an elderly carpenter, a just man. His wife was younger—she was his second wife—and something of a contrast to him; a dreaming woman, devout but in a different way from her husband. She loved such stories as that of Hannah. For him the prophets, with their message of righteousness, were his strength. The boys took after him: upright, stable. All save one: he was hers in every way, though he and his father worked together admirably, and he never stirred from the shop until the old man died last year. Then one day he was gone and on my asking one of the family, I was told that he had said that he must see Yohannan bar Zaccharius, the son of the old Levite, who has made such a stir by becoming a Nazarite and preaching this purification from sin by immersion in Jordan. But he didn't stay long with that band of prophets. I was told that leaving them he crossed Jordan and disappeared into the desert itself. I thought of him much. He'd always given me the sense of being born to some destiny. His brothers would make better citizens: but prophets are always alien. So one day, catching sight of him in the street here near his mother's house, I stopped him. It was clear that he must have undergone some considerable hardship, perhaps some ordeal. He was—how shall I put it—less human. To my question where he had been he replied from the prophet Hosea, 'I will allure thee into the wilderness.' My reply, 'Have you found Him whom the heart seeks?' caused a short silence followed by, 'Yes,' and then again more slowly, 'Yes.' I felt that he wished me to question him further. 'Son, has He given you a sign?' Again that slow 'Yes.' I waited, and he did not move. Then in so quiet a tone as though he were speaking to himself unaware of me, with his eyes on the ground, as if to recall every incident of a memorable scene, he began.

" 'Into the desert for there I knew I must be answered, be challenged. God lets that other Power ask us questions, to try us, and we, with the help of His Spirit in us, must find the inspiration to reply. In these answers, which spring out of the heart given Him, we find His Voice has spoken to us. As the Jordan water touched my forehead, I knew my mind had been opened as Isaiah's mouth was opened by the coal from the altar. I knew who I was. But being That One how should I act? I fasted the better to let the mist of appetite clear from the mind's mirror. Then when hunger came I knew the first question. If I were he who should deliver, should I not, by the power given me, preserve myself? The desert had no food but it had pebbles that looked like bread. Should I not will them to be what they seemed? But if I were indeed become one with the Creative Will why should I have to be a wizard, making loaves by magic? Surely I should live directly by the Creative Word which now I knew had begun to speak within me. The miracle of the corn turning the earth we cannot eat into bread is meant to be matched—not eliminated—by the miracle of God turning the body, which is first fed by bread, into the Soul which His Word feeds.' He paused.

"I said, 'Son I believe the Spirit of the Most High is with you. Said It more to you?'

"He continued hardly seeming to notice I had spoken. 'My message then was all that mattered. How could I, coming from this place, speak with authority to those who must hear and live? Power to provide for myself I should not and need not use. But the Power might open my way to the hearts of others. Whether from the fasting or no I felt a wonderful lightness. That may have brought the picture into my mind, the vision of God's messenger. . . .'

" 'Him Ye look for shall suddenly come to his Temple'? I quoting asked.

" 'Yes. Surely that would be right? There would be no violence, only an arrest of the people's attention? To descend directly, say from the topmost pinnacle of the Temple itself? But ought I so to force the occasion? Do the

Scriptures in any of the prophecies say that the messenger will come down out of the sky?'

" 'The Daniel prophecy,' I answered, 'says the final Judge will come on clouds of glory in the heavens but that is the end of all things.' I do not know whether he heard me.

"He went on: 'It was a second test. The third then was inevitable. If I would not use the spiritual power for myself nor to impress others, would I use no power at all? If I would not employ spiritual power, would I also refuse to use physical force of any sort? The Prince of this world has offered me his Kingdom to do with as I will, on one condition—that I use his weapons and so become his liege man. I have answered, I am the Son of the Father in Heaven. It is He that will justify me, not I myself by force of arms. To do that would be to show I doubted the position my Father has granted me.' "

The old man made no comment on these remarkable words he quoted. After a silence, I asked him: "Surely Rabbi, if these are his decisions he will have the Spirit of the Most High with him? He rejects magic for himself and for others and equally he rejects the temptations to use violence."

"I believe," he answered, "such were the convictions that came to him in the wilderness, and I hold with you, and am grateful for your agreement, that he set his feet upon a path where God can be his guide."

My old guest was silent but I saw his speaking had not brought him relief. He was still troubled in spirit. "If you believe that then it is well?" I said with a question in my voice to draw him further.

The old man's trouble broke. "Has he fully and finally found? If so, can he point out the way, or is he precipitate, presuming? Oh, Sir," the old man turned to me with tears in his eyes, "forgive me if our hunger and thirst for the

Most High should make us presumptuous thinking that of His Great Mercy he might visit us, the lowly and outcaste."

"His promise is," I could comfort him, "that with the humble and the contrite He chooses to dwell."

"Pray He grant that our humble trust in Him may save us. But, as Malachi says, He tries His servants as a smelter refines ore. Now I am in the fire of that trial. May the All Merciful have mercy."

He was silent so long that I put out my hand to him in the dusk. "Will you not, Father," I asked him, "come and break the evening bread with me. My servants have prepared for me at the inn." He arose with a bow of courteous assent. Together we walked down the twilight street across which faint glowing bands of light spread from still open doors while, lying at the lower end far away, gleamed like quicksilver the still lake reflecting a sky, cloudless, sunless, starless.

When my servants had left us after serving our meal, the old scribe, who had eaten in a silence I respected, continued as though only a pause had come between his last sentence and this; and indeed our minds must have been holding to the same theme throughout our silent supper.

"I could not speak with him more because the sun was already in the west and it was the day of preparation for the Sabbath. When we were all met in our small synagogue the following morning I was giving the reading from the Torah and the Bar Joseph, as one of our leading families, sat near by. This young Joshua was naturally there also. I could not but notice that when I turned to the people and holding the sacred roll called to them the great 'Hear, oh Israel,' that while the others listened with quiet docility or a few bent their heads in deeper worship, Joshua threw his back with his eyes shining. Indeed, I even thought he was going to speak. But the Invocation ended, and, passing the roll of the Law back to the two servers who received it in its wrought coverings, I waited a moment in silent supplication, before turning to our reading from the prophets. We are very informal in our small place of worship. So, when on looking up I saw that Joshua had taken hold of the roll of the prophets—it lay in readiness on the broad balustrade between my seat and the people's first row of benches—I did not ask it back. He was evidently searching for a passage. On finding the passage he stood up and began to read. I sat still, for the passage he had chosen was one of the greatest of the promises—it is indeed my favorite reading to my flock—the promise that Messiah shall not come as a scourge, no, not to the oppressors, but as a deliverer of the people from their sins and their ills. His voice—you have heard it when he is moved?" I nodded. "His voice is wonderful. It does not shake but it shakes something in the ear and heart of every listener. He read the words, 'The Lord has sent me to bind up the broken, to loose the bound, to heal, to proclaim the Day of the Fulfilled Promise'; and his voice rose with each proclamation until every head in our quiet, good, sleepy-stubborn flock was turned to the reader.

"He had so declaimed the passage that it was no conventionalized, long overdue promise but something being offered here and now to anyone who would accept it. I could see the bewildered, half-expectant, half-protesting look on my hillside fisherfolk's faces. I could hear even whispers of half-roused protesting curiosity—'What's that?' 'Who's this?' 'It's carpenter Joseph's son back.'

"Then across the rising whispers Joshua's voice struck. He turned to them: he spoke slowly and calmly. 'Today, here and now, this long promised thing has happened. Now at this moment at this spot it is at last fulfilled.'

"There could be no doubt of what he meant. The congregation rose as one man. He walked out, the people swarming after him. I followed and there they were going along the street that leads to the steepest part of the little bluff on which this village of ours is built. He was half leading them: they half dogging him. Suddenly I saw them make a lunge at him. I don't think they quite knew what they were doing or what they in fact wanted. He had roused in them a kind of intolerable question and they had to put him to the test, to press some meaning, some clear answer from him. Anyhow he could lead them no further nor retreat from them any more. He was at bay—a precipice behind and this blind flock hemming him in, pressing him back. I was by then on the outskirts of the crowd, and as the street goes down steeply to the cliff edge I could look over the scene. At that moment he suddenly opened his arms to them, and they, seeming to fear such a friendly touch from one they wanted to push away from them, gave. And he with outspread arms walked through them while they withdrew on each side of him. He passed me without seeming to see me, but Jacob his brother, who had been hanging about at the crowd's edge, then caught up with him. They went back together to their mother's house.

"I didn't see him again for some time and (oddly, I thought) none mentioned him to me. So one day as I was passing their house I called in. The men were still out at work but the mother welcomed me. I asked her where Joshua was, and watched her face. Across it came, or rather deepened, not a shadow, not an anxiety, but a wondering question, a hope shot with disquietude. 'He is so unlike the others,' she said, 'I am thankful to Heaven that they are so sound and upright. But he is more, far more.' 'Do you think he believes he has the prophetic call?' I asked. 'Yes, I know it is a great thing for a mother to say, but I do believe that he feels and knows it.' 'Where is he now?'

'He left after that Sabbath occasion. He is gone down to the big cities on the lakeside yonder.' 'Have you heard of him?' She hesitated. Then looking at the ground she said almost in a whisper, 'Wonderful things; he's healing, preaching to crowds, curing possessed. . . .' She stopped. We sat in silence. Then I heard her repeating the words from Samuel, 'He has visited his people.' I rose. 'We must be open to catch sight of the signs of his coming,' I said, 'but we must guard against presumption disguised as hope.' She was not listening, nor did she ask my blessing as I left.

"Her report, however, was amply confirmed in a few weeks. Stories of all sorts were passing up and down the village street. Once again these simple people were clearly of two minds. They were intrigued and daunted, upset and proud. Their village becoming famous was something against those big, clever trading towns. That one of their least successful fellow villagers was bringing such fame, that was not so pleasant. So when one day it was said that he was coming back for a visit, the village was really moved. He entered the street with quite a crowd behind him and our home crowd moved down to meet them. As soon as they were within earshot a tall man walking near him shouted out. 'I was lame.' 'You look lazy,' shouted back someone among us. 'I was blind,' came another shout. 'Shamming blindness is easier than working hard.' 'I was possessed.' 'You don't look any too sane now.' Our Nazareth crowd was now laughing. But the others laughed, too, and more merrily. 'Your man's fine,' they called out, 'why not let him try on you!'

"That led to a silence. The two groups were now opposite each other with Joshua standing between them. 'Come,' he said, and I thought that there was a new ring of authority in his voice, 'I'll help anyone who wants helping.' He was certainly quite sure of himself and this made the crowds look at each other. 'He means it,' said one of his side. Then someone said, 'We want better weather for the crops and the fishing. Can you get it?' 'Why do you want it?' he asked. 'Isn't what the Father sends good enough?' 'That's clever, but he's hedging,' another said.

"Then someone ran back and in a few moments returned with our poor village idiot. 'Cure him, Rabbi!' 'Do you really want him cured or do you want a show?' The voice was stern and there was an unpleasant silence. 'Do any of you love him? Would you be glad to have him as your equal? Isn't he more useful as a beast of burden?' It was shrewdly said. His father let the poor creature out as a kind of pack horse to carry loads up the hill. The crowd—it was now one—shifted uneasily but Joshua stood quietly looking around.

"Out of the whispering I heard a woman's voice calling, 'Come back I tell you. Don't go mixing with strangers.' A small child had toddled out, but coming opposite Joshua he stopped, turning his face up to him. You couldn't tell if the child were looking at him, the eyes squinted so violently. He looked down and the grimness left his forehead. 'Poor baby,' Joshua had taken it up in his arms, slipping his left hand over its eyes. He seemed to forget all of us milling around, and was whispering in the child's ear. After a moment he held the child out at arm's length and laughed while he laughed back. Then we saw the eyes were straight. The boy ran to his mother. 'Why, there's a wonder,' she called out pleased at the notice the crowd was giving. But the child's father growled. 'A fine miracle! That brat squints whenever you shout at it. I warrant tomorrow it will be squinting twice as hard at my first oath.'

"Some laughed, others tried to hush him. An old half blind man who had an ague stumbled forward. 'Can't you do something for my ache?' he asked dully. Immediately Joshua bent down to him. The crowd went silent so I could hear: 'You need not be in pain if you do not wish to be.' 'Don't wish to be!' 'Do you think I can help you?' 'I know I want you to.' 'Very well.' 'It's stopped, like an abscess breaking, it's stopped.'

" 'There! There!' shouted Joshua's partisans. Back came our critics: 'Oh, that's only old Jacob's ache—it's always coming and going.' 'Rabbi . . . ?' began someone else. It was cut short by a sneer. "*Rabbi?* Why don't you call *me* Rabbi? Who is he? He's the jobbing carpenter's jobless son! Working weak miracles with those who don't know you is a far sight easier than making sound tables for those who do!' The laugh that rose at this was cut short by Joshua's voice. 'Very well,' Joshua was using the same phrase that he had used to old Jacob, but what a terrible difference intonation can make, 'you can explain away everything, even the finger of God and so you make His fatherly power ineffective.' As he spoke he turned and went down the hill.

"He never has come back, though once he was near by in the next town. There, he had such success that the hamlet was overrun. They pressed round on him as though they were fascinated."

"Yes, I have seen that," I confirmed my old guest.

"He was in the yard of one of the cottages but you couldn't have got to him through the press. People were around him as bees around their queen at swarming time. He spoke on and on until up here we heard of it and, calling me to accompany them, his mother and brothers went to him. 'He's inspired,' people were saying. And the flood of language was astonishing. His voice rose like a tide. We could hear him over a hundred pointing heads though we couldn't get near enough to catch a glimpse of himself. He was telling them of the wonderful time which would come if they would only believe what he taught. Jacob turned to his mother, 'This is really too much. He'll be saying next that he's the Messiah and we'll have the Romans beating us all up within the week.' 'I think you'd better try and catch him,' she replied nervously. 'The sun must have been too much for him.' They sent a boy to make his way through the crowd. The boy must have got through, for the eloquence stopped and only a sharp shout of challenge came. 'Mother and brother want me, you say! I say I have no mother or brother except those who do my Father's will.' The crowd began to move. Evidently he was leading them off. Miriam and her couple of boys looked helplessly at each other. 'What will happen, Rabbi?' she asked turning to me. I could not comfort her for the same question lay unanswered in my heart."

The old man fell silent. There was no one in the caravanserai but ourselves and already my two servants were drowsing near the door. I arose as my guest gained his feet. At the doorway I told one of the men to see him home. As we parted he said, "Sir, seek him out and ask him whether and how he knows that he has the Eternal with him. He would not listen to me, I know, but you sit in Moses' seat and surely he will answer you even though he may not obey."

I promised I would not leave Galilee till I had spoken with Joshua of Nazareth.

Chapter III

WE REACHED the large trading town of Capernaum the next day by noon. Certainly the fame of a new prophet had made our search easy, at least it was easy to get in his tracks. He was, we were told, actually at that hour preaching in one of the city houses. But the fact that it was easy to trace him made it hard to come up with him. The crowd was so dense that it had spread out from the house over the street. One of my men found that a lane at the back of the building led to an outside staircase which ran up to the roof. Already a group ahead of us had found this access and had gone up to the roof itself and begun stripping off the tiles to get a view down into the yard at the back of the house. I paused by a window which gave me a sight of the whole covered-in interior. The place was packed, and not with the rabble only. A number of scribes were seated listening as Joshua spoke. Whether or not they wanted to leave did not matter now because no one could get out; the door was blocked with human bodies. The Rabbis did not look very happy for Joshua was laying down the Law just where it might challenge them most. Nor was he paying them the professional courtesy of quoting a passage of the Law each time when he made a sally at their expense. Still less did he follow the ordinary good manners of referring to the finding of some earlier Rabbinic authority. Indeed, time and again he would say, 'I tell you' and 'I know' and this manner of address was to such men, tied by their scholarship and quotation of authorities, almost as galling in its style as in the substance of its attack. The crowd, on the other hand, was, naturally, as pleased and as noisy as an audience in a cockpit.

So engrossed were we all that it was only when a shower of brick dust fell on their heads that they looked up. We all stared then. For those men on the roof who had stripped off the tiling were actually lowering a mattress through the gap, and on it, precariously descending, was one, obviously a paralytic. Joshua alone appeared to take such a dramatic intrusion for granted. As the pallet at last swung down safely at his feet he simply remarked, "That's enough. Your sin will let you go." No one spoke in the tense silence. Then, with that sudden change of tone, "You over there," he nodded at the scribes, "you're saying to yourselves: 'This is blasphemy. No human being can loose another from his sins. Only God can forgive.' Let us put it to the proof. I say I am the man of men that God promised He would send to set men free. So, can you not see, it's just the same whether I tell this lad to use his limbs again or whether I say to him, 'The sin that's tied you up is gone.' The proof that the Absolution is real, that I am what I say I am and can do what you deny I can do, is that the lad is cured—you cannot deny that. Well, boy, come along. Up you get and clear off with your mattress."

The crowd was so taken aback that somehow the lad squeezed his way out and, as half went after him to gape, Joshua broke off his discourse. But though he had certainly healed a very sick lad and one who, it was clear, needed just that insight into what was wrong, my learned colleagues caught none of that contagion of health. They soured under his rebuke and he lowered at them. The two, the prophet and the guardians of the Law looked at each other in complete misunderstanding. I went down the steps and as I went my heart sank faster.

My mind was now made up. Speak with him I must. I had heard quite clearly from my vantage. And far more significant than the boy's healing was the healer's explanation. I had heard him use those fateful words which were under every man's tongue in those days—"*Bar Enas*"—"The Son of Man" of the Daniel prophecy. There could be no manner of doubt that he was convinced that he, Joshua bar Joseph, was Joshua bar Enas the Delivering Son of Man. Of that I was certain. My one remaining doubt was *which* deliverer?

The people were looking for the Messiah. But we, the scribes, knew that two were foretold—or at least that two Messianic fulfillments were possible. The prophets had offered us two hopes. My own school of Hillel, though we were too discreet to preach openly what was unpopular with the masses, held that the conquering Messiah of the One Hundred and Tenth Psalm had come with Judas the Hasmonaean and passed with his degenerate successor. Had not the Eternal shown that that was not the path? But another was promised: one who should be a peaceful Teacher and Healer of his People. The Zealots would have none of this. They called it defeatism, escapism, treason to the Holy Faith and Blood. But the holiest men I knew had held this conception. There was realism in this outlook too. The Maccabees had failed. Our own forces, in military terms, were contemptible. Rome spread over the world's face. Within her Empire men might serve God as they pleased. The crafty Procurator had made the Imperial position unmistakable. We could carry on as we liked in our religious life and in our social practices. Indeed the whole of our civil and religious life was left to us provided we left the military issue in the hands of the conquerors and so long as no one under the guise of religion raised a political revolt. It was a fair offer to those who really cared for the religious life more than for politics and power. Naturally the politicians would never give a sincere promise to respect this compromise, but, as clearly, the Roman was hard and definite. It came to this: any claim to be a political Messiah was treason. One had only to show that one made that claim for his execution to be assured.

My visit, I began to see, would not only satisfy my own need to know whether God had once more raised up a prophet in Israel. It might also be given to me to forestall a hopeless rising and a bloody repression. I might save a devoted man for a life of inspiring teachership and wonderful usefulness if I could speak with him and get him to clear his position; to clear it, before misrepresentation should have aroused the Roman suspicion, or opposition among his own people have driven him to extremes.

Certainly I had no time to lose. After leaving the house where the lad was cured my men and I went to secure our lodging at the hostelry. It was a well-appointed place, very different from the empty arcades where we had spent the night before up in the hillside village of Nazareth. As I was dining, one of my two companions who acted as my confidential messenger, a faithful servant of long standing called Joab, came to me.

"The man you have come to inquire into, Master, is," he paused, "debating again."

"Where?" I said rising, for we of Hillel's school eat sparingly at noon and I was determined to miss no opportunity of learning all I could of how Joshua's mind was tending.

"He's dining with one of the big tax farmers here."

"A tax farmer!" Here was a new strange light. No man who was seeking popularity would or could be seen in such company. All sides were against these leeches. Even the Romans, who set them on our flanks, despised the bloodsuckers and often let them be mobbed.

My servant guided me quickly to the house. It had the appearance of wealth and was close to the merchants' quarters. It also had, as it needed, good strong walls, high barred windows and a massive door. But the door was open today, and we went in with a stream of people. It was certainly the oddest sight a tax farmer's house could ever have presented. Tables were set out in the courts; for a feast was in progress and everyone seemed welcome. In the central place of honor sat Joshua.

"That's the tax farmer himself on the preacher's left," said my servant. He certainly was a mean-featured little fellow, but that cunning lean face had all its crinkles curled into smiles. He was obviously in the highest of spirits. His eyes were always on Joshua, but he would keep on jumping up and capering about, plying people with food and drink and telling the servants, who looked quite bewildered, to bring more. While we watched he came skipping down among the tables, patting guests on the back, calling out to others and always, like a bird, twisting around his head to catch a glance at Joshua. Joshua, too, always seemed keeping an eye on him and to be ready, whenever the little fellow flicked around, to give him a grave smile.

As he came near the door, one of the guests shouted out, "Why this blowout, Levi?"

"Oh, because I'm happy."

"Well, I suppose that's a reason for going all out. You used to be the gloomiest, richest grind fist in the ten cities and now you're getting merry by going broke."

"That's it," Levi shouted. "Come in, come in. The more the merrier. A good fire's the best for garbage." He reached us and had laid hold of me with the same childish glee.

"Come along, join our feast. It's my birthday." His head flashed around to the head table. "There was I, hard at it making money: right at it and as gloomy as Hell. I'd half looked up: 'One more damned peasant short on his payments, I'll be bound. And cursing me who has to pay the Romans,' I was saying in a sort of routine growl.

"I put out my hand, and looked up, for it was taken. He literally put me on my feet, looked into my eyes, and, bang, I knew what I'd always wanted. Before he'd said, 'Come along,' I was coming. 'Let's have a feast, Master, just to blow the whole cobweb away.' 'All right,' he smiled. He's no spoilsport. Look, he's smiling at me now!"

And pulling us along he started pushing to the head table. "Now here's somebody for you to convert, Rabbi," he shouted out. "You turned a bloodsucker into a merry madman at a glance. What about turning a word spinner into a soul winner?" Joshua looked up at him smiling and then, turning to me, the smile did not so much fade as set or settle into the eyes. He was searching me as I was searching him.

Whether he would have questioned me I know not. For at that moment the hubbub at the gateway to the court changed its tone as a busy hive changes its hum when interference is suspected. I saw Joshua's eyes turn and become fixed. Half a dozen scribes in a close group were investigating the scene. I recognized a couple from the morning's meeting. Their presence had so chilled the gaiety that across the gap I could hear their clear supercilious literary accent.

"A Rabbi, and claiming to be far more than any humble scribe or careful keeper of the Law would dare to claim; yet, after the great Declaration off to a disreputable merry-making with the riffraff of the town."

Joshua's remarkable voice carried back without his raising it in the slightest. "Where would you expect to find a doctor? Surely not wasting his time among you the healthy but in the slums. My mission is to the failures, not to the spiritually successful." If he were trying to gain their assent he certainly failed. Assuredly they could never have welcomed an outsider coming in uninvited to do work they had neglected or failed to accomplish. They were good according to their narrow lights, loving the Law. They could not understand one who broke its details to extend its span. I wondered whether he realized that. I wondered whether he had any more understanding of their limitations than they had of his enthusiasm, limitations just as pathetic in their way as the limitations of this noisy, good-hearted, disreputable crowd.

Anyhow the spirit of careless good fellowship was gone. Little Levi himself felt it: "Now, gentlemen, if everyone's finished we'd better be clearing up. I have a few things to settle in the house before leaving town." He bent down speaking low to Joshua. They withdrew into the main house and there was nothing to do but to leave with the dwindling guests.

I stayed in Capernaum a week trying to have a conversation with him. But it was never possible. He went about with a crowd and on its fringe were always those upset, embittered local clergy. They followed him with a kind of exasperated curiosity. He was now healing right and left and his teaching was the very heart of the Law. The crowd grew every day. And as his success mounted I think he grew careless as to whether the clergy understood or not. On the Sabbath he was in the great synagogue. I am glad to say he did not try to speak. Most of the people there were watching him. The atmosphere was ominous; many were hoping for a scene; the clergy and some of the richer folk were nervous but resolved to call help if there were any disturbance. Only Joshua seemed unaware of the tension. He worshiped with complete absorption and, at the close, I could see that the relief at there being no disturbance and his obviously deep reverence had, if not soothed the authorities, made them less apprehensive.

All was spoiled, however, that very afternoon. He took the permitted exercise in the fields near the town, and some who were following him began to pick the half ripe wheat, rolled it in their hands and ate it. Of course a purist, on the lookout for a breach of the rules, challenged him. He chose the occasion once again to claim that dangerously ambiguous title, *Bar Enas,* and to say that he being so had as good a right to infringe the Sabbath as the hungry David had had to eat the shewbread. Could he have thought that the simple punctilious officials could accept that? The defense was more provocative than the act defended.

Nor did he fall afoul only of the old conventionalists. That next week there was a fast and the followers of his own preceptor, the Nazarite Yohannan, were fasting as well. Certainly there was nothing conventional about their abstinence. It was they, this time, that challenged him for his followers' looseness. "Why can't you make your crowd show a little discipline?" they asked with some exasperation. Their exasperation certainly was not lessened when he told them that they could fast if they wished, for they had lost their leader. "And so will my lot should they lose me. Meanwhile, naturally, as they have me they are gay. What have they to worry over? Besides, when the wine is at full ferment, you can't bottle it except in new skins that have a lot of give in them. If you put men, as happy as these are now, into straight stiff rules, they'll just break the rules, ruin the code and be thrown away themselves." True enough it all was, if he had been starting fresh with really new people. But there was the Holy Law and the ancient rulings thick upon it, and these people were, though mixed and loose, still the People—the Law was theirs and the promises theirs, the Covenant theirs. I wondered, then, if the break really came, on which side would they be found? On his, the gay defiant liberator, who was really teaching them a far harder way, or on the side of the old stiff venerable tradition, stiff but just, heavy but shaped by centuries of wearing to the shoulders that carried it.

I decided to stay on for one more Sabbath at least. As the week wore on the tension grew steadily higher. Wherever he went crowds swarmed, and the larger the crowd the more his power and his personal emphasis seemed to increase. Healing seemed to run through whole rows of his listeners, as all kinds of diseased people were pushed into the front. The scene when he was doing this was terribly moving. There was the mob egging him on and roaring at each success. There were the patients groaning and crying out for his attention and then yelling for joy as recovery came upon them.

Often, too, the crowd would suddenly writhe. The dense pack of people that had been pressing until they were almost one body, would give, as when a storm of wind flattens ripe wheat. But Joshua would stand his ground as out of the gap, left by the shrinking mass, that living corpse, the leper staggered and fell, moaning for aid. And as the creature tumbled at his feet, Joshua would stoop, raise him and placing his hands fearlessly on the corrupted flesh, would shout in triumph, "I will you to be well! See, the scurf is falling off and there is clean flesh underneath. Let him go my friends, let him go. Off to the priests my man, as Moses has commanded. They'll certify your recovery." The crowd would gasp, shudder and then cheer.

A couple of blind men then fumbled their way forward. Even while they were still trying to grope their path toward the voice, Joshua had come close, reached in and drawn them out. One glance at each of the blank questing faces and, taking the elder (the bleared eyeballs rolled helplessly), Joshua cupped his hands round the beggar's ears and bringing his own face within a hand's breadth of the other's, spoke low, but with such intensity that the crowd was spellbound. We could all hear the shearing emphasis with which he was saying, "See! See! You can! You know you can: You know I can make you see. Now listen to me: I *will* you to have your sight back now, this moment, *Now!*" At that *Now* the beggar's jaw fell. I have never seen surprised delight smite a human face with such shock. The eyes fluttered, then swung to a true focus onto Joshua's, which drew back slowly, still holding the man's total attention. Another moment and the poor bleared lenses were washed with a flood of tears. He staggered back swinging his head in every direction: at the sky, the crowd, the earth. He plucked at the sleeve of his garment, picking it up with thumb and finger. His infant sight was next caught by the look of his hand itself. He turned it to and fro like a new object of the strangest appearance. Indeed it was so to him, for this was the first time that he had ever seen that which till now had been his one contact with the world. His eyes began again to look over the crowd; sometimes his face broke into a grin, again he was clearly quite at a loss. The crowd began to play with him. Joshua's voice checked the fooling. "Someone who has had sight all these years have the common goodness to lead him to his home. Don't you see, he's lost in the world the Father has given back to him." The crowd sobered. A couple came forward to lead the man away. As he turned to go with them, Joshua called after him, "And now take care how you see. Seek to see the Father guiding your every step."

The second blind man had a woman following him. Joshuas' treatment in this case differed. After that first deep look, he drew the man to him, running his fingers round the eye socket and, all the while, as far as I could hear, asking him questions in a low voice. Next he turned the man's face to the sun, swinging the eyes to and fro in the full blaze. I could hear the man's cry of "Oh, oh" as he twisted himself out of Joshua's hands. The woman who was standing trembling behind him caught him. For a moment they looked at each other quite oblivious of the surging crowd. Above the noise I could hear his cry, "It's you, you." Joshua was among them at a stride. "Son, now you can see the devotion that guided you all those dark years, don't forget the love that has given you back your sight. Don't lose your way in this garish world, your way back to your Father's home. He has given you your sight to help you find your way there."

They disappeared in the crowd and Joshua turned, pointing his hand to where the mass was densest. "That man there," he cried, and the mass ejected a poor creature whose every gesture revealed his helplessness. One did not have to listen, in the expectant hush, to the mutilated sound, almost a howl, that came from his mouth, to know that he was a deaf-mute. As soon as he was within arm's reach Joshua laid hold of him, thrusting his fingers into the patient's ears but saying nothing, looking only into his eyes with an intensity which made the creature blink. Then, quick as a conjuror, the powerful hands swept round and he had hold of the lolling tongue, working it, the lips and the throat muscles as a potter works clay. As he did so he nodded affirmatively at the man. It was clear he was answering the silent question with tremendous emphasis,

"Yes, I can and will heal you." But as this cure was not instantaneous the crowd, which was gaping ready to roar at a new success, began to join in, shouting out encouragements, comments and even jibes. Joshua continued, undistracted by the babel. Suddenly cutting through the confusion, a shout stilled the clamor. "I can hear. I can hear. I can hear you breathing."

"That's a good beginning," replied Joshua, "but you must go on. You must learn to listen to your Father's voice speaking in your heart. Take care that the new sounds that you can now catch don't drown that voice. Better, then, that you had stayed deaf."

"I'll remember, master, be sure I will," the man said over his shoulder. Already he was pushing away to enter the new world open to him. "And don't forget what you say matters even more than what you hear. Above all take care of the new power given your tongue. It's what comes out of you that can really mar you or make you." But the patient was already gone and I saw a shadow of disappointment cloud the generous good will on Joshua's face.

Beside these sick, there was always a pack of maniacs shrieking and foaming, reaching an extremity of violence, calling him by every possible name, even the Sacred Name, then rolling on the ground and as he shouted out his commands coming up gasping and sane. Of course I've seen many exorcists and healers but never such a storming success. Whenever the maniacs shouted out that he was the Son of God, he called back, "Hold your tongue." But I noted that he did not disown the title. Naturally, many of us Pietists have sons who, when young, practice exorcism; (the power seems to leave them after marriage). And I have noticed that maniacs frequently read what is in the exorcist's mind especially if he has on his mind a special problem. As these Galilean maniacs howled the Holy Name I wondered whether Joshua already were wondering if he might not be more than a prophet, yes, more than any one of the prophets had foretold.

The authorities could hardly help being alarmed. A centurion or two were on watch but they were far too interested to interfere—such a show was a relief, I suppose, from ordinary police patrol work. The clergy wanted him told to move on and to get out of town. But of course there being no breach of the peace, the military authorities did not act. It might have been better, had there been some cause for official action. It might have prevented a worse end. Certainly it was during those days that the gap between the prophet and the church opened until no bridge seemed able to span it.

Indeed that last Sabbath brought the issue to a head. He was again at the synagogue. All might have gone well, but this time a man with a withered arm had come in and was deliberately trying to attract Joshua's sympathy and attention. The clergy noticed it and were of course nervous, it being service time on the Sabbath. Would Joshua provoke the issue then and there? Or would he tell the man, who certainly had had the disability for some time, the arm being twisted back to the body, to come the next day and be healed? Joshua took up the challenge in a way to put the clergy on the defensive and in the wrong. Calling the man out, he turned to the officials and asked them if it were right to do right on a Holy Day in a Holy Place? Of course they had nothing to reply. He clinched his argument against them by saying that they certainly wouldn't leave one of their valuable farm beasts in a ditch if it had tumbled in during the Sabbath. The illustration was not quite fair. The beast well might be in great distress and die if it were not taken out. They should have asked him, with all courtesy, whether the Sabbath should be kept and how; whether the command that it should be holy would require one to postpone work which could be done as well on another day. He might have made his ruling clear, so they would have known where they stood with him. But, as was to be expected, they were angry and flustered at his refusal to treat them with consideration and he caught their irritation. He who had spoken so beautifully on the mountain side in the spring morning of the Father's unlimited love toward all and of his patience with all, now in this crowded city place was returning anger for anger. He who with open hands of healing had walked through a mob, which was trembling irresolute whether to lynch him for his presumptuous claims, and yet was melted the next moment through his demonstration of good will, this man now offered not love but defiance. Granted we Pharisees and scribes had fallen from that passionate search for the Holiness our fathers possessed, still the guarding of the Sabbath was surely to be excused in us. There in Galilee so little stood between the simple people and the corruptions of the Gentiles. If the Law was given to Israel that it might be a peculiar People, then the outer rails of the Holy Place needed preserving, and the Sabbath itself, as Moses declared, was one of the ten central laws of the Covenant! No Sabbath, no Israel.

Once more, after this crisis, I made an effort to speak to him. But the crowd was so dense about him and those rough Galileans were openly obstructive to one in a scribe's dress, that I had no choice but to desist. They thought my only purpose was to interfere with him. My one desire was to ask him a single question, a question as grave for me as for him: Did he know whither he was going? If I could not speak with him I had not the heart to stay on. Miracles are of little interest to those who seek first and foremost the Eternal and His Kingdom.

And such is tragedy, that it was his unqualified honesty

even here that broke down the last possible bridge between him and the orthodox. There were evidently a few men of wide understanding among the Capernaum scribes. Though they were sprung from the common people many a country scribe, such as my old friend of Nazareth, were true scholars and brave if pious thinkers. Indeed I knew of one or two of these Rabbis by name. As my holy grandfather came himself from Babylon, it was natural for me not to confine scholarship to Jerusalem. Had we not Philo the Pious, moreover, at that time in Alexandria?

One of these Capernaum scholars, Abiram by name, was following Joshua as was I. He was bolder than I. Perhaps he felt the urgency more, the desperate need that this acute problem be brought to a head. He must have had some authority with the people, for in a lull during the healing he quickly made his way, without too much opposition, into the front row of onlookers. I could hear him, though I was at the back; he was evidently determined all should hear his question.

"You have spoken strangely, challengingly, dangerously. You have healed but you have also broken the Law. Who are You? Who are You? Are you using these magic powers to lead people astray by making them believe that it is safe for them to disregard the Law? How can we know that evil has not given you a wizard's power to act as its decoy? Cannot Satan make himself look like an angel of light? Prove who you are! Healing can be magic. Ask God to give you the power to show an unmistakable portent and sign of authority from Him." He stopped. There was a silence. Some were impressed. Many no doubt hoped for some prodigy, for some great event, an earthquake, a lightning flash from the clear sky.

Joshua's voice broke the tension like the crack of a whip lash. "Your sons exorcise—are they in league with the

Devil? A sign: the teaching and the healing are the sign. A portent! Yes, you want that. You are the evil ones calling evil good and able to misapprehend the finger of God as the imprint of the Devil. You've proved so utterly unfaithful to your vows that you've lost the power to recognize the touch of God's hand. Indeed, you're so unforgivably depraved that you can't be taught, you can't be saved, you will never be forgiven."

I turned away. How could I hope for anything now. Could I dare to win him, to work with him, to discuss with him after this? Maybe I should still have striven, but the party I had to serve was now cut off from him and to so great extent by his own act. As to staying and listening to the rising protests of the local scribes and Pharisees, how well I knew what they had to say. How true and yet useless, how inapposite. Must priest and prophet always make the uncircumcised to triumph?

I decided, then, to leave early the next day, so as to get far before the noon heat. But though up early, the city was seething by the time we were mounted and set for the southern road. And as I passed the space where the town streets converge to become the country highroad I heard a voice raised with an amazing power. People were running in that direction and as I looked from the saddle I could see over their heads the figure of Joshua. His arms were raised and his voice, telling at any time now carried a terrible emphasis: "Woe, woe, woe, to Capernaum. . . ." And then followed town after town where he had preached. The denunciation was unstinted. "They have refused to repent. They have been called to salvation and have rejected it. They have been shown signs and wonders and yet have refused to believe. If such works had been done in Tyre and Sidon those heathen and debauched cities would have repented at once in dust and ashes. Sodom and Gomorrah, cities of unspeakable evil given over to the infernal fires, nevertheless their inhabitants should be faring better than these Galilean towns when God would judge man." Not only my narrow-minded country colleagues were to be utterly condemned and cast into the outer darkness, even the stupid, greedy, open-eared crowds were to be doomed too. My spirit faltered. With a bitter foreboding I set out for Jerusalem.

Chapter IV

ON *RETURNING* to my chambers in the Temple precincts I found, almost at once, that my absence had been noted and the reason for it discovered.

I was to lecture that day on the Law. My favorite pupil had come to carry the rolls from which I should read the standard commentaries. His was a dark, passionate nature, a wonderful mind but moving so quickly and deeply as often to disarrange his words before they were ordered. The sonority of the Hebrew language and thought, in which high feeling moves as the harmonics in a noble bell, was confused in him. He had been brought up in Tarsus of Cilicia and, though still hardly a man, had in his early years there contracted a great deal of the overrichness of late Greek thought. That thought had departed from the pure love of the Wisdom, which Ben Sirach and my grandfather's predecessors had loved. It had taken to those curious sophistries, those Gnostic spiritisms and those sinister twistings of carnal idolatries into dark and bloodstained mysteries. Such subtleties, wherein violent emotion is blended with overwrought thinking, can be handled all too well in that tongue which moves with the glittering flow of a snake passing over a rock, eddying around every obstacle and opposing to nothing the definite and unyielding impact, the measured and firm impress of the human foot planted on the rock. Hebrew stands: Greek evades.

Yet Saul was a passionate Jew. All his wrestling with the

subtle Hellenistic mind only made him recoil the more violently to cast himself almost frantically at the foot of the undeflectable Law. Often I have seen him in agony, as he spoke of the Law's unwavering righteousness, and when I would read to him from the prophets and the Psalms of the Eternal's Fatherly love for His People, how His compassion to the contrite is as unfailing as His Justice to the wicked, of His infinitely gentle understanding of our frailty, Saul would cry, "No! No! only sacrifice can appease Him, only Blood can atone." I would quote Micah and Jeremiah showing that the sacrifice which He requires is our contrition, and how our showing mercy obtains mercy for us from Him, Who because He is so willing to pardon we may dare call our Father, the All Merciful. Yet when these moods, almost maniacal in their violence, were upon him, nothing could assuage his terror.

Today, however, he was almost spritely in contrast to my own dejection, and it was with a certain hint of amused malice that he said while he stooped to gather the rolls: "You must not spend too much time today with us poor convicts of sin, Master, trying to win us to the light and peace of forgiveness. You are needed for higher and more helpful work. The High Priest himself is asking that you wait on him as soon as you return from your Galilean tour of inspection. He needs light on certain happenings out among those half-breed borderers." I said nothing, but again foreboding took my heart.

After I had taught I went to the High Priest's quarters and asked if he would see me. I was ushered in at once. Caiaphas was then at the height of his power. Tall, domineering, a born administrator, his able face was stressed and marked with a permanent anxiety. A man, to whose pride finesse, still more dissimulation, was gall, years of negotiation had left exasperated. No Zealot hated more the conqueror, but the realism of his intellect and the strength of his will kept him to his inflexible determination never to strike unless the blow could prosper. His control was shown now. We had never been intimates. Far too different were our points of view and our spirits. His was that of the man absorbed in power and its devices: mine has ever been that of seeking by dedicated learning to draw nigh to the Eternal. But he valued scholarship as giving prestige to the Temple. Though I was his junior and not yet elected to any office, he treated me with the courtesy due my birth. On my side despite my shunning his proud and restless spirit I could confess that apart from his own prestige he did cherish with a passionate if narrow devotion the Holy Place. And today he went beyond courtesy almost to friendliness, he drew me to a window embrasure, asked me to be seated and after inquiring after my health and remarking I was tired, said with frank directness that he had heard that I had been up in Galilee making inquiries about a disturbance there.

"Those Galileans," he said with a bitter laugh. "Always the hem pollutes the garment, always they are causing trouble, even by getting themselves slaughtered here in the very Temple, defiling the place with their mixed blood and giving the tyrant by their crude fanaticism, an opportunity to begin a massacre in the Sanctuary itself. Believe me, it will not be the orthodox who will bring ruin on this place. These northern violent fools, unsound in observance of the Law, irreverent to priests and scribes, these are the very men who will involve us in a hopeless issue with our oppressors." Then with a sudden turn and a direct question to me, "Who is this Joshua of Nazareth?"

"I've seen him," I answered. "He is certainly a healer of outstanding power: a preacher of deep beauty when at peace: a man of unmistakable devotion, uncommon authenticity, but. . . ."

"He was first with Yohannan bar Zaccharius, the Nazarite, wasn't he?"

"Yes, I understand he stayed either with Yohannan or somewhere in the desert until the Nazarite was seized by Herod."

"I knew old Zaccharius, of course. Children of old people are often strange. What do men of today, in modern times, want to be aping Elijah and the first prophets! It's a species of play acting. But apart from that, whether he was theatrical or no, he did at least keep to the proper stage, the desert. This Joshua, however, is raising disturbances even in the big towns, I hear?"

I told him what I had seen and learned.

His face darkened. "He breaks the Law: he lives as comfortably as a merchant but does not work: he denounces the rich like Yohannan, but will not strip himself—I hear his raiment is finely woven. Did not I say it! Here is a typical Galilean! Always stirring up trouble, yet, while making the occupation army press harder upon us, the shield of Israel, these rats gnaw at the inner side of our harness."

"He is more, far more than a Zealot."

"He heals! Well, some of your own friends have had healer sons and exorcist nephews. I know little of such things. My task is to defend the Holy Place, preserve the practice of the Law, perpetuate the sacrifice, but you Pietists are always claiming such results. Don't be offended. I am not saying that such gifts may not be granted. The Holy Scriptures attest them in the past. I am saying, even if it were true that this Joshua can heal, by whose authority does he do it, and what does it prove? Certainly no right to flout the true authority."

Here was the same challenge which I had heard uttered

by the Capernaum Rabbi. Evidently, though, Caiaphas had not heard of all that I had seen, and I saw no reason to tell him what would not have enlightened him but rather would further have darkened his mind with suspicion and dislike. Therefore I only said, "He is good and gifted and may indeed be great. But he needs help and when the country scribes thwart him in his spontaneous wish to be of use, he cannot understand them and is bitterly grieved."

Under his beard Caiaphas' mouth twisted. "You Chassidim are always overlenient with those who brood upon the prophets and give grudgingly what they must give to the ever Holy Law." Then with a flash of scorn. "This mage I am informed not only is obeyed by the powers of sickness and by the Devil. He orders the elements as though he were Elijah, whom, no doubt, he thinks he is."

I said that I had seen nothing of this magic nor indeed heard of it.

"Oh, he's still cautious I expect." Caiaphas' voice became cold. "But the Sanhedrin must know what is going on in these Nazarenes' minds or before we know it, he'll be at the Temple doors proclaiming, God forgive me, that he is the Messiah come to announce the new age. Heaven knows, we have had enough of this thing. We ought by now to have learned our lesson. The one object of the Zealots is just that, to get the Temple embroiled hopelessly with the Romans. Pilate is a pitiless man but no fool. Caesar would not have left him the task of holding us down for a longer term than any man has been able to hold the praetorship, were he not as crafty as he is hard. I know that type. We understand each other like the lion and lion hunter. Neither will strike until he is sure that his blow will go home. I will not have my hand forced by ignorant fanatics. I will not see Israel smitten a crushing stroke which the tyrant himself is loath to deliver. If this Galilean Joshua is thinking about imitating Theudas and that crowd my mind is made up. . . ."

"I can answer from my own knowledge that he is certainly not thinking of copying the Maccabees. . . ." I began.

He cut me short. "It makes no difference who his exemplar may be. . . . You think none too ill of him?"

"I repeat, he is a healer; deeply concerned with human suffering and always anxious to cure it. The only fault I found in him was a hasty exasperation with those guardians of holy forms who would have him choose a proper time and place to bring help to the ill or mutilated."

I had completed now all that I could say. As Caiaphas led me to the door, he closed our conversation with the ominous words, "Well, whatever his gifts and whoever he may think himself to be, if you have any influence on him," he paused, and added, turning on me that tense searching look of the over-anxious ruler, "I tell you, charge him that he come not to Jerusalem."

Chapter V

I *WAS* glad that on my return to my chambers young Saul was not there. The sense of inevitable tragedy—of that terrible conflict between the old discipline and the new liberator—made me desire to be alone. The boy was quick to see one's mood and, like all young minds of highly nervous intelligence, he was apt to sense it and then in some sort of defensiveness, to attack. He wanted, I believe, reassurance. Certainly the slightest sign that his master was in perplexity made him take the offensive, in order to see whether the rock on which he wished to rest blind faith could have in it any flaw. Blind reliance or ruthless defiance were his only possible rest points, all in between was for him an agony of unbearable indecision. His teacher must either be a disproved fool or divinely infallible—discredited or deified.

I could not get the Galilean poet-prophet out of my mind. When I took a codex of the prophets to gain from their clarion faith a wind to scatter my doubt, I opened on the Servant Passage in Isaiah. I know, of course, that this passage refers to the Holy People and to their rejection by the world and the suffering they must undergo if they would be God's patient witness. But my gloomy thoughts first traveled down the ages asking what in fact our witness had been. Had the priest and the prophet both cared and cared only for the Eternal and His love and peace, would the prophet have been stoned and the priest have become, like Lot's wife, petrified, a pillar of bitter salt instead of a well of living water? Could these two voices have spoken in unison, would not the world then have listened? Were we always to be doomed to confuse the life-giving eternal word of the Lord by bitter personal dispute and internal controversy? My mind then naturally came to the immediate concern. Were not all the early prophets northerners? Was not Caiaphas himself the typical priest whose very virtues of inflexible performance of the Law and absorption in the duties of administration provoked always the prophets' contempt and denunciation?

Caiaphas' words were still ringing in my ears. But were not they themselves a prophecy? He might have spoken them as a sincere warning. But did not those words foretell a destiny too great for him to deflect, though he might be a dreadful instrument of their fulfillment? As surely as the stormy waters of Galilee must rush through Jordan down to the Dead Sea, bitter and still, so inevitably must not this the latest of the Nazarites, the last of the prophets, be swept along by his own impetuous current until he be engulfed in the ecclesiastical system which he could neither disregard nor escape. I had been told to act upon the warning to keep Joshua away from the capital. But how could any human force deliver him from the doom of his office? Where must a prophet end, where must his career be ended save in Jerusalem?

Days passed but neither disregard and forgetfulness nor any solution came to release my mind. I could not suppress the memory of Joshua; I could not doubt his beauty and conviction and the great value that his message could have if only he could in every respect fulfill it in his own actions. Neither could I deny his increasing lack of understanding and charity. His voice, at first lyric, had now become polemic. Must it not end with an ultimatum. All I could do was, through my position, to keep track of his movements.

I did not flatter myself that any message that I might send him would fare better than those personal attempts that I had made to speak directly with him. My new friend, the reader of the Law, from Nazareth itself, sent replies to my inquiries. At first I was relieved by the tenor of these. True, Joshua had become more violent and stories in circulation about him had grown to be extremely disquieting. He had appointed twelve lieutenants, as though he were creating new tribes. These he had sent out on a mission tour which had gone far to split the countryside into two camps, those for him and those against. Wherever these missioners were received, all went well, perhaps all too well. Healings and exorcisms were almost as common with the lieutenants as with their leader. But where they met any criticism, any unwillingness to receive these men on their own extreme valuation, then the village or town was cursed and warned that it would be destroyed by fire like the Cities of the Plain. Perhaps to give point to this threat, which if vain in boast was frightful in intent, stories evidently similar to such as Caiaphas had heard, were circulated, how that Joshua not only was a healer but a weather wizard. These lieutenants boasted that not only did he walk about on the lake at night as though the water were a floor of marble, but once when they were all nearly being capsized in one of those well-known Galilean whirlwinds, he so aptly told it to clear off that they swore it was his word that scattered the wind. On the other hand, to encourage his own side, stories as fantastic if less harmful were spread of his power to feed, literally thousands, from the few scraps of food his lieutenants were carrying. A leader who could provision a force of five thousand by magic, or can persuade them somehow that he can, is, need it be said, one whose movements might well disturb military minds far more easy-going than Pilate's. I dreaded whether the Roman might already have found as much reason for suspicion as Caiaphas himself.

Then just as all Galilee seemed about to be ranged in two exclusive camps and a small religious war to be launched, suddenly, to the relief of all of us who both loved the man as long as he spoke of the love of God and dreaded with all our hearts religion involved in an issue of violence, Joshua left the country. He was reported to have crossed the frontier, to have gone out from the Holy Land and to be living definitely among the Samaritans and Syrians. Outside the fold, living among the Gentiles, how could he preserve ceremonial cleanliness and, so discredited, he would be of no further concern to our authorities. He would—as did many Galileans—have lost caste and be lost and merged among those magicians, sorcerers and soothsayers who infest the mixed Greek and Arab populations. Stories of healings still trickled through. He was then apparently ready to welcome people not of the Blood as his followers. Indeed one report said that he was making friends with the Romans themselves; that he had cured a noncommissioned officer's child without even seeing it, had told the Centurion that his faith had made his child's recovery possible and that faith, faith such as this fighter had, faith which was the one thing needed for salvation, this foreign soldier possessed in a higher degree than he, Joshua, had found in any Jew.

For a little while this fact gave me a species of comfort. Should he quite discredit himself with the strictly orthodox, then the danger that the extreme claim, which I increasingly dreaded that he must make, could rouse any following or anything but contempt, would be past and over. My last report declared that he had been lost sight of. There had been the usual series of healing stories, of Gentiles also coming under his spell and of his yielding to their entreaties, though at first he seemed to have told them that his message was not for them. Perhaps, I speculated, he is thinking of finding his mission outside Israel. After all, that might be the solution of the prophetic problem. It may be the prophets are sent, as the tale of Jonah says, not to their own people but to the great world powers, whether Nineveh or Rome, to tell them, as the Law tells the true Jew, that God is their Father and that His Law of Righteousness also binds them. When the silence continued, my mind changed and I concluded that the enthusiasm of the excitable borderers had, as so often before, evaporated. But I was wrong.

Immediate work, however, will drive out ineffective concern for distant troubles. Those who then served the Temple had much to keep them from brooding on the morrow however enigmatic. Perhaps it would have been better if we had given more time to reading the signs of the times. Then the ship of Israel's fate might have been guided more by the stars of the Eternal than by that opportunism, the eye of whose concern never lifts beyond the problem of rounding some particular rock of difficulty. The more precarious became our position the more impossible did it seem to find any time for long views, the more pressing grew innumerable temporary decisions.

One day the whole problem was brought back to me. I had, beside Saul, a number of young men of position who treated me as a spiritual counselor. One of these was in complete contrast to Saul. He lacked my Benjamite's zeal. Indeed his sunny nature seemed to have no sense of conscience as an accuser. I think he had no reason for such a feeling. He was not careless in the unwise sense. His was one of those natures who found it easy to be kind, who have a sense of the goodness of life. "Ezra bar Kantheras," said one of my colleagues, "is one whom Adam's sin seems almost to have missed." Certainly he was generous, happy, open and courageous. He used to come and see me with casual ease, not anxiously asking advice but telling me as a nephew might tell an uncle all his plans and occurrences, discussing everything under heaven—what scrolls he had been reading, the latest horse he had added to his stables, the rebuilding of one of his father's country houses, for his family was very wealthy and his father had lately given him one of these for himself. Lately he had also, with the same openness, told me of his oncoming marriage. Again his fortune held. His parents and the parents of his spouse were close friends and had desired the match, I knew, since the two were children. He was deeply in love, but this passion, too, was clear and bright as a child's joy with its possessions. He used to tell me about their future with the vivid assurance of a boy telling his father of a picnic they would have tomorrow. The overclouded national sky he hardly seemed to notice. He certainly was not without a deep love of his country, his religion and his God. But he felt that they would surely see that his happiness would flower and fruit as it had already budded. He kept the Law, loved to keep it, felt it was natural to observe it, was proud of it. . . . Was he not of the People chosen by God to have and preserve His Covenant? And therefore in consequence his Heavenly Father would bless him with prosperity and happiness. Had he not so treated, so honored and obeyed his earthly father and had not this earthly father so treated him? Could his Heavenly Father act otherwise to His dutiful child? He loved beauty, goodness, and truth, he felt they were of his nature and of the nature of the world his Father had made.

One day, however, when I looked up, as he stood in the door asking if he might enter, a different face met mine. I had never before seen it clouded. "I thought you knew the secret of how to be devout without being dismal?" I thought the smiling jest would rouse him. But certainly the smile faded from mine when, instead of answering my question, he asked me another.

"Master, have you ever heard of a Galilean teacher. . . . ?"

"Joshua of Nazareth?"

"You do know him?"

"How do you?"

"I told you my father wanted me to rebuild the house we have above the Esdraelon Plain. He has told me to make it into a building that will endure for his great-grandchildren. It is to be the home in which his grandchildren are to be reared. Everything is to be beautifully enduring. My betrothed is to have a home worthy as a setting for her children. So I went north to Lebanon to get the timbers for the roof and the wall panels. When up there I thought I would ride over to Carmel. The view over the Great Sea is wonderful. . . ."

"I know it . . . it always reminds me that the Sea of Eternity flows out beyond our fretted lives."

"Yes, and of Elijah and his decisive victory of the faith against the idolaters! I was out there. I'd left my small company at the foot of the steepest climb, had clambered up and sat down to take in that vast view. The sun had begun to western and the unwalled floor of water was a pavement of incandescent sapphire. That view of the Great Sea, when there is nothing but light, space, and splendor, always brings back to me that awful moment when we are told that Moses was permitted to see the pavement of sapphire on which the Shekinah itself shines. And somehow at that instant, young and happy and blessed as I am, something happens. I feel happier than ever but there is a strange longing in my happiness, a small alien piercing note begins to sound at the very heart of the vast peaceful harmony. Usually I rouse myself and shake it off. I know there are men who have fled into the wilderness and some have come back with a message from God. But I know my duty is to live among men, to raise up seed to Abraham: to be a righteous steward of our family's great wealth with which God has blessed us. God has shown me, hasn't He?"—I did not deny or assent—"that He intends me to live this life now and by so living fully I shall be made ready for the life to come. When my children's children are raised up I can then ask that I may rest with the just." He paused. "I don't know," he began again slowly, "whether it was the sacredness of the place or whether I was looking at life more extensively than usual because of my oncoming marriage. I know, whatever the reason, that as the strange joy with its longing at the core began to form in my mind, I did not banish it. I let it grow, attending only to the current that drew me out, not to the cable which strained as it would hold me to the shore. Suddenly the outgoing force laid hold of me. I was seized with an unbearable longing. All my plans, all my life seemed far worse than childish. I was a creature playing in the gathering twilight, in the dust with straws and if I raised my head a moment, as I saw I did at these moments of vision, there, sliding past, was a pageant of such splendor, such a glorious company calling me to join them, to leave the gathering dark, to enter with them into the life eternal.

"I don't know how long I stood there, my physical eyes blinded by the physical splendor and my soul stunned with the glory of which light is but a shadow. I don't think it was with any shock that I became aware that another was standing beside me. I don't think I asked why he was there or who he might be. I believe I hadn't even noticed that he had begun to speak. The words seemed more in my mind than in my ear, so perfectly did they seem the thoughts, and nothing but the thoughts, that such a scene, such an experience must form. I cannot tell you a word he said, though he must have used language; it was so utterly apposite that it seemed not a man commenting on God's works but the works themselves finding voice." He paused, his boyish eloquence having exhausted him.

To give him time I interjected. "Yes, no human being I have ever heard has ever spoken more in the very tone of nature and so perfectly with its rhythm."

Ezra did not seem to have heard me. He was living again his ecstasy on the cliff of Carmel. His voice came to him again. "He must have asked me something, I suppose. I know he read my immediate pressing need. I turned from the flood of western glory where, as with Elijah's prayer, the heavens on fire seemed to have made the water itself pure flame. My companion was still looking at the glory. The flood of light struck upon his face from above and below. The eyes shone like chrysoprase. The skin seemed glowing with an interior flame. The hair was like a nimbus round his head. 'Good Master,' I cried, 'what shall I do to become possessed of this Eternal Life?' I saw it beating all around us and flooding through him. He smiled at me and to his majesty was added gentleness. Surely I felt he would let me in, too—he would lead me out on these still peaceful splendid waters. This was heaven's gate: 'Good?' and he was asking me a question. 'Why call me good? Only He in whose perfect presence we stand, only He is good.' My question still remained haunting me: he saw I couldn't answer his till that was answered: so he went on quietly, 'You know the Law. It is the Law of Life, not of Death. Our Father gave it us to lead us as a sure path to Him and who finds Him finds the Eternal Life. You know the Ten Steps whereby He has made a ladder for us to His very feet.' 'I've kept them all from a boy,' I said with a sudden delight. Though I have always prized it most highly never had I understood before the full preciousness of the Law. His eyes, which had been gazing into the sun's deluge, drinking in that flood without wavering, now turned on mine, for I was watching him with the delighted anxiety with which a child awaits the last sentence in a wonderful story. Those eyes aflame, yet with a radiance of pure gentleness, were seeing into depths of my soul hidden even from myself. After a while he remarked, 'Yes, only one thing is lacking. You have given our Father a joyful service and so He calls you to a higher position, to follow Him, freely delivered even now from every limitation. Your riches now can only hinder you. Sell all of them. Give the profits straight away to those who still need possessions, to the poor, to those too poor to be able to think of the supreme treasure that's now within your grasp.' At that he put out his hand and laid it on my shoulder. I have never been so touched. A thrill of life ran through me. I felt an amazing love fill me. I knew he cared for me greatly, though it seemed almost unbelievable that he should. 'Come, be free in this service which alone is freedom. It is so light a service when you are free from other burdens. My way is straight and simple. It leads directly into the Father's Kingdom on the coast of which you are standing this moment. I'll go with you. We'll travel there yoked together.' He had put his arm over my shoulder. 'Come along. Do you see down there, in the fold of the hill, next to the combe where the track goes and your attendants are waiting?' I followed his finger and saw a small company. 'The little flock which the Father has given me to lead into the Kingdom. Join with us. I promise you, the frontier is now at our feet.' I had been looking at the unlimited radiance, where land, hills and valleys, stones and pitfalls had all been melted in a liquid radiance. And now the earth looked dark and dismal and that little company a sorry knot of tramps, dusty, pointless, shiftless. What could they do with the world? What had they to do with unearthly radiance I had glimpsed? Why! They, none of them had troubled to climb the ridge and watch the splendor. I could see them now clearly. One was absorbed picking a stone from his sandal or mending its thong; another rolled on his back like an ass just freed of its saddle; a couple were gossiping; one dozing; another pair munching bread unwrapped from a knotted end of their tattered robes.

"I did not dare look with my recovered sight at him who had called me. I did not dare, lest he, too, should seem to have been robbed of his splendid power and become simply an eloquent peasant. I did glance out to sea and already the sun was shorn of its sky-filling glory. It hung a majestic disk passing far away, sinking into the west, sinking into the ocean which darkened to receive it and along whose dark waters now only a narrowing lengthening path of gold stretched as the one bridge between retreating heaven and the darkening earth. A huge sorrow seemed to swell up from those waters and flood my heart. I had wanted to believe, but how could I? Was this really the answer to that wonderful question that had risen in me? Where was marriage, the place of just power, the home and children, the arts and knowledge? Where were all these, in so simple a solution? Oh, believe me, had he shown me the path I would have gone. In my moment of disappointment, as in my moment of ecstasy, all my personal hopes had shrunk to nothing. But if I were to forsake mankind's way, I must be sure of the other! Did he really know? Or was he but a poet of terrible power, of an awful appositeness, able to question the soul to its depths but unable to answer life's actual question?"

There were tears in his voice and eyes when he ceased. I rose and drew him down to the couch on which I had been seated.

"Ezra, I believe you have met one of the prophets—one who, maybe, will be remembered with Isaiah and Jeremiah

—greater, I would venture to hazard, than Elijah of Carmel, the founder of our prophetic line."

"You do know him?"

"I have been under the spell of his inspiration."

"But does he speak with the prophet's authority?"

"I believe he does. By that I mean, I believe he speaks with the authority of the seer, of one who at those moments of open vision sees into the Kingdom of the Most High."

"Then I should have followed him, left parents, left my affianced wife, left my position, power, and responsibilities!"

"Ezra, if you should be ill one day and go to one of our great physicians what would he do? Two things: first, as the great Greek physicians say, he would diagnose, he would look right through you and gain insight into your condition. He would tell you what your painful symptom, that drove you to him, really disclosed. Then he would prescribe. He would first say, you are a human being ill of this human disease. Next he would remark that you were of such an age, situation, particular disposition. To one he would give a diet, to a second a strong drug, to a third massage and baths, to a fourth bleeding or opening and excision of diseased tissue." Ezra looked puzzled. I then added, "All I mean by my little parable is that seers, whether of the body or soul, have a double task: to describe disease and to prescribe its cure. I do not say that Joshua the prophet does not combine both gifts. But it need not be so. A man may be a wonderful diagnostician and his actual treatments may not be so true. That does not disprove his diagnosis." I paused, reflected, then decided to go on. "Joshua may have been right, may always be right in his prescriptions, as I believe he is inspired in his diagnosis, in his sense of our one illness, lack of God's presence. But if your conscience, and not your convenience, tells you that his prescription was as yet not for you, do not I pray dismiss his diagnosis. Whatever you do with your life, and you may well do much, do not forget, I beg you, do not forget that longing, do not forget that moment when longing drew you up to the window of vision. However elaborately, however long you live, do not lose your way: see, watch, search, that every step, however diagonally the staircase goes, leads you up the mount where is revealed Him in whose Presence there is life."

The boy was gazing at the floor. His question, though, showed he had heard. "But should men give up their duties —office, rightful positions, the magistracy and the home?"

"Surely there are, we see from the Scriptures, two callings. The prophets are summoned to become the channel of the voice of the Most High. For them to have any other task but to wait upon His summons and repeat what He utters in their heart, would be to distract them from their sacred vigil. But they are few. For the remainder of us, we serve Him in the many offices He has prepared for us, passing, as it were, from the altar of marriage to that of the Law and from the Law to the Sacrifice. The eye may do nothing but see: the hand may turn itself to many uses."

"Then I may marry and not do wrong?"

"Assuredly."

"But have I missed the way to Eternal Life? Is the gate closed? Why did he press me to go at once?"

"Did he not say keep the Law and you have the Life Eternal? Perhaps he wanted to test you that he might see, and you might see, where actually you are. The Eternal Life is yours by God's covenant with His People. But some enter into it here and now, as it were, with a leap. Others go by the stages of a full life and are only born fully into it at death."

Ezra had risen. His cheerful vitality was brimming again in him.

"Thank you, Master. Your words have cleared my way. I'll never forget Carmel. It is a beacon, not yet the actual lamp to light my next step."

"I believe so, my son. Go in peace."

But when he had gone, my own peace did not return. How authentic had sounded that interview on Elijah's mountain. True, the youth could not accept the call. His hesitation had proved his unreadiness. And the call itself? Yes, that was the authentic question. But beside the call, an answer was proposed. Was that the answer? John and all the prophets were in the desert; they were the conscience of mankind, the voice of God speaking from outside the world, putting the Eternal question and leaving man's heart to answer it. We in the service of the world strove to give men actual earthly answers to the Eternal question. But Joshua with his little troupe was in the world but not of it. What were his real answers to marriage, money, the magistracy? Was he just waiting for the world to end? My heart went out to him. The question he asked we all yearned to answer. My mind misdoubted, for I could not see an answer in his advices. Must not he himself find such inadequate, and make some move, some tragic move, to bring to an issue his hopes and the actual problems?

I did not see Caiaphas for some months, save to catch a glimpse of him, hastening through the outer courts, striding to protest to Pilate about some fresh provocative brutality of his troops, or, to preside over his committee of the Council. That executive group now sat nearly every day, debating how best for that moment to throw our helpless weight, with the Herodians or with the Zealots. The Sanhedrin was already divided by the pressure of work into such committees. Caiaphas naturally presided over the executive. My interests and use lay with the judiciary and the educational. Not till the early summer would I have reached forty and so be called upon to sit in the full Sanhedrin itself. Nor, had I known what to counsel, could I have come in upon their problems without neglecting my own. As the Greek has said, the cobbler must stick to his last. But he might have added that we all have to wear and be worn by the cobbler's notion of a shoe. I was lecturing every day to students for the Rabbinate, to those entering upon their Levitical duties, to classes formed by visiting members of the Diaspora, to study groups of proselytes. Never had there been such a desire to study the Law, such a spirit of reverent inquiry, such a need and demand to carry on the holy work of the Chassidim, of Ben Sirach and of all the lovers of wisdom, and of my revered grandfather Hillel. The spirit of the Most High Himself seemed to shine with His Shekinah—now vanished from the Holy of Holies—on the Holy Page of the Law, bringing fresh wisdom and understanding at every perusal. From Alexandria Philo the Pious sent us a stream of thinkers. Indeed so widespread and so earnest seemed the desire to seek out God's will that those who did not lower their eyes from the sacred text and look out upon the troubled seas of violent men might have thought that because the sun of Eternal Truth was so clear in the sky, the voyage of the Chosen People was nearing some haven.

Then, my teaching work finished, I must turn till midnight to the many rulings sent to me for confirmation on points at issue: between Sadducee and Pharisee; between the Law and the Ritual; between justice and equity; spirit and letter; on innovations and adaptations; on the laws of marriage among those living among the Gentiles; whether fees be paid for Temple services and, if so, must rich and poor pay alike and must these payments ever vary. Moses knew nothing of money and therefore of interest or fluctuations of prices. Before the Most High I can say that though I spent part of every day and every night on these issues,

issues which could and did split righteous and God-fearing men into hostile camps, I never found one such dispute in which the right was wholly on one side nor one which could be answered with a clear conviction that this was the only answer evident and obvious arising straight from the Law. How can men denounce and go to war when even a human judge can see that no actual issue ever gave an absolute mandate to disregard the opponent's claim!

The spring had begun again to send its first messengers north before I noticed its signs. My last lecture class was gone and young Saul was rewinding and replacing the rolls in their cylinders. I had gone to the window. The afternoon sun was now pouring through and my eye had been caught by a gleam of emerald in the tide of gold. It was the first frond put out by the fig tree whose branches were trained around the casement and the leaf seemed to shine as clear as a piece of beryl. The Passover would be upon us shortly. Another year had gone around and, still a captive, Israel was once again to celebrate her deliverance from Egypt. Coming to the window I could look down into the street which led up to the Temple's entrance. It was densely crowded. All those of the Dispersion were gathering for the oncoming festival. Men of the Holy Race were coming up with camels from the East; African visitors attended by Negro slaves; Jews from the north with tall blond servants; men, clearly seafarers who must have landed at Joppa from the far west, from Rome, even from Spain, but a few days previously. Israel, like a net thrown out into the ocean of the world, was now drawing in to yield its tribute to the Most High.

I stood silent for some time thinking of this unique paradox—of us the Chosen now always wandering among the nations who seemed so assured and so settled. But it is the empires and the nations who vanish from their mighty seats and it is the People who have nowhere to rest their head and seem as dust driven from the feet of every new conqueror, it is the suffering People that survives and is indestructible. My thought was given a twist into words when at my shoulder Saul's voice said,

"God is compelling His People to spread themselves over the wide lands of the Gentiles. He has scattered us like seed among the nations that we may the better proselytise them. So shall we conquer those who think they have conquered us."

The hum from the street came surging up like the blended cries of the sea birds when at their nesting time they fill the cliffs of Carmel. Then the tone suddenly changed as when a sea hawk swoops among the birds. Concerted shouting was beginning to rise from the further end of the street where it turned out of sight. Already those moving about immediately below us were glancing back up the street, and two or three of the soldiers stationed at the Temple Gate I saw looking from the top of the steps over the people's heads. One of them turned back quickly into the small guard house. A moment later he ran out, carrying spears and a cluster of slung shields for himself and his companions. The shouting grew louder, and now everyone, where the street widened before the Temple steps, had turned around waiting to see what was coming. Amid the hubbub I could catch a word, the word. I turned, but Saul was already watching me, no longer the street.

"Another Messiah!" he said bitterly. "And another massacre! If these peasant fools, these vulgar Zealots won't take advice and informed leadership why in the name of judgment must they choose this time to pollute the Passover with their mixed blood?"

The soldiers now had their spears aligned, and had sent back one of their number, no doubt to call for reinforcements. Once more the war cry arose, "Now for it: now for it: strike and free us now, Son of David." Around the bend in the street came that first run of rabble, that always like pariah dogs, circle round a stampede. Then the shouters themselves came in sight. Nobody had arms: not even a bludgeon. Some had armfuls of palm fronds which they scattered on the road, others threw their cloaks into the dust. Out of the middle of this little crowd of enthusiasts emerged a man riding on a fine onga. He also was unarmed. The soldiers could now see as clearly as we, and as clearly were at a loss. This was no uprising; it was a kind of performance, a small pageant, a charade. My attempt to make out what this queer little procession might mean and my fear of what it might lead to, stopped, ruled out by a stronger feeling, sheer astonishment. I could see the rider's face—it was Joshua's. I could see it so clearly in that strong light, as he looked up at the Temple, that I could detect on it an expression I had never seen before. Previously I had seen him angry and winning, desperately earnest and humorous, gentle and denunciatory. Now he was none of these. He was rapt like a sleep walker.

"So that's it," I heard Saul's voice at my ear, "he's not going to make a dash for the Temple with a band of long-knife men. He's going to try to get in by fulfilling the Prophecy peacefully. A clever piece of stage management, if it were not rank blasphemy. He thinks he's fulfilling Zacharias' "Look for your king as one of the Melchizedek rulers peacefully entering on his office mounted on the judge's proper steed the white ass!"

My ear listened to Saul's shrewd interpretation. My mind noted the contemptuous hatred that charged his words. I remember reflecting on this Benjamite's bitter scorn for all who were not of the pure blood. But my eyes were watching the rapid issue in the street fifty feet below us. The soldiers were reinforced but still hesitated to charge this odd but unmenacing cavalcade. The shout that rose from it was certainly the old cry, "Up rebels, up." But no small traveling troupe of circus performers could have been less political, less military. Yet the cry was treasonable and at this time and place there could only be one answer. I saw the spears swing down to the ready and the Centurion raise his vine stock cudgel. When that fell the platoon of legionaries would sweep through the crowd like a scythe swathing down fresh grass. Anyone unable to get out of the way would be run through and rolled down into the gutter before a cock could finish his crow. There was perhaps time for five heartbeats, though mine seemed to have stopped. Then the whole thing was over—the scene was shifted as by a miracle. Suddenly, while the Centurion looked across at Joshua and Joshua still stared fixedly in front of him at the Temple, from a side street a train of camels none of us had noticed and whose drivers had been unaware of the scene they emerged onto, swung across the small open area between the onga and its little crowd on one side and the waiting soldiers on the other. As the great swinging beasts, broad with their burdens and towering with top-hamper, pushed their way along, the onga shied, wincing at their rank odor, and as a swollen saddle bag struck its muzzle, the animal bolted. With a quick stumbling scramble it bore its rider back up the street. Some minutes were required for the long file of draft beasts to progress across the area, and for the caravan's trail of followers—some of whom a moment before had taken up the cry of revolt—to pass out of sight, and finally for the traffic approaching to the Temple to resume its current.

I heard the Centurion call out some rough jest to his men and they wheeled back to the guardhouse at the head of the steps. A couple of minutes later everything looked as though the strange drama we had just gazed down upon must have been a hallucination. I breathed again with a sigh of relief. Saul's only comment showed a harder heart, if cooler nerve:

"Next time the penalty of blasphemy will not go unexacted."

"But," I said, "he was coming as a messenger of peace. That is why he was saved. That gave the Centurion pause and gave time for that providential accident to throw him back into safety."

Saul's face was hot with suppressed violence. "Master"—and once conventional courtesy was at an end his rage broke—"don't quibble with the Sacred Law. That peasant is a blasphemer set on leading the ignorant to destruction. He deserves to die and he shall not escape the judgment." And my tempestuous disciple burning with zeal for the Law, without the conventional leave-taking required when leaving the presence of a teacher, strode away.

Chapter VI

NEXT MORNING when we met, Saul was in a better mood. I saw I was not now to be denounced, I should be treated with a semirespectful irony. It was clear that something had pleased him; but that was far from saying that anything had softened him. Things had obviously gone his way. But that boded no good for others when his mood of righteous indignation was still upon him.

After my lecture, even before collecting the rolls, he had to tell me of his good news. "Caiaphas may be no scholar, and often in his obsession with work I have known him scant the full observance of every tittle and jot. But he has our holy interests at heart and he, at least, will endure no parodies of Holy Things." Then coming to illustrative detail of a fact which he knew I was as well acquainted with as he, he went on. "Caiaphas heard of what had nearly taken place on the Temple steps when the people were gathering for the Passover. I repeat, bloodshed at such a time and place is itself a blasphemy and had things gone forward only bloodshed could have prevented something even worse taking place."

"But," I interrupted, "it was all providentially prevented."

"God does not intervene to save those who break His Commandments. The doom of this blasphemer is not prevented, only postponed for graver punishment. Caiaphas sent at once two trusted servants and they have traced the false prophet. He's lying up in a little village just outside.

No doubt he's biding his time to repeat again what yesterday proved a fiasco. He is staying in the hamlet called Bethany."

"Saul," I again interrupted, "you know I am as sworn as you to be a guardian of the Law. And now I speak as your teacher. Take care that behind your outward zeal a fatal pride may not be pushing you on. Watch yourself that when you believe and protest that it is God's glory you are jealous for, it may not be your arrogance toward all that cannot see the righteousness of a Pharisee. Search in your heart and see whether in its depths there does not lurk an angry fear lest our advertised holiness, our care for every item of the Law may be a covering to conceal a major and basic deviation. You are always speaking of God's Justice. I seldom hear you speak of His Mercy, and you are not merciful. Beware lest His Mercy should lay hold upon you and make you worship, to an extreme that you believe is impossible, what you have despised, the spirit of the prophets. Remember the threefold demand made on us by that spirit of the Most High. To deal justly is but the beginning: to love mercy and to be humble are the central and completing terms of that commandment. Ask yourself are you fulfilling these requirements of the Eternal?"

For a moment I thought he would protest. But he was always a disciplinarian. Did I use the language of a gentle father or an elder friend, as I commonly used with him and with all my pupils, in this his present mood he would have challenged me rudely enough. But now I spoke as a doctor of the Law and as his acknowledged teacher. He paused. I heard him muttering, "Always the prophets, and the Psalms—weakness, sentiment. . . . " But as I stood before him, silent, waiting for his obedience, he gradually bowed low and went away in silence.

Left alone, the more I thought over the incident, the less

desperate I felt it to be. I could not say whether what we had witnessed had been accident or design. I still cannot be sure whether Joshua had become footsore and weary in his journey up to Jerusalem and one of his companions had borrowed a mount for him and then, as they followed him, someone had started the rousing chorus; or whether he himself had been trying deliberately to create a new part, the peaceful Messiah, and to test out how far this new non-violent approach of the Prophet Messenger could be received by priest and soldier. If he believed in peace as I had heard him preach with such moving force, then he might well hold that if he came in peace openly asking to be received in the name of God's righteousness, compunction would open the hearts of the officials and the gates would be opened for the meek forerunner of the King of Glory to enter in. I could not say, but I did feel increasingly assured that with great courage he had tried out an original and daring venture. The sudden intervention and solution of the crisis might well be taken, by a sensitive soul such as his, as a heavenly sign to show him that he had done, at least for the time being, all that was required of him.

Indeed such was my wish to believe this, such my faith in his considered and expressed conviction that the Eternal is the King of Peace and only allows violence to cancel out violence, that when going out the Temple courts next day I noticed nothing amiss. There were the crowds common at that time of year, seething in the great Court of the Gentiles with the clamor of Babel itself. You might hear forty tongues spoken at once and Hebrew being quoted in such outlandish accents that the sacred words seemed parodied and profaned. Worse, you might see Temple officials wrangling over the exchange rate at which foreign coinage could purchase the official Temple shekel and involved in disputes with recent proselytes which rose almost to violence. These angry cries and gusts of dispute mingled with careless but irreverent laughter, with people's shouting to each other to make themselves heard, with the blows and curses of the cattle herders and the bellowing of the sacrificial beasts. This pandemonium was always a misery and a mortification for many of us at the Passovertide. How one longed for some quiet country synagogue where out of a sacred stillness of silent worship, as a rainbow over a quiet lake, the holy words of the Law rose linking man and his Maker in the recitation of the Sacred Covenant. Yet could we expect our poor People, scattered like shepherdless sheep over the waste earth, preyed on by wolves and coming back but once in their life to the fold—could we be surprised if on arrival they were not as docile and patient as we would wish? They had had to rebuff the wolves out in the wild. Under their tough coats they had cherished a dream of peace. One day they would enter the one Holy Place in all the world. They would see and hear and smell the home of their hearts, the place which all their lives they had longed to see and which year by year had grown in their homesick imagination until no earthly precinct could ever be such a haven of peace. There, they could not help believing, there they would find a welcome from their happier fellows who dwelt always under the Law in the calm of the Eternal. They would see at last living holiness. They would meet with a loving-kindness and a communion not to be met anywhere else, for it would be extended to them by those of their brethren whom the Heavenly Father had chosen, because they were like Him, to act as His hosts to the less blessed, the less good. Instead what they found were harassed administrators anxiously and irritably trying to sustain a system itself inadequate to meet the conflicting demands of patriot and conqueror, of reformer and conservative. Where could these hurried and anxious officials, men absorbed with means and compromises and contriving, find place for these poor hungry outsiders. How could the servants of the Temple look upon these pilgrims as other than a source of income. As souls they were only an embarrassment, crudely ignorant of all the real problems which beset a religion wherever it actually touches the earth. These strangers, daring to criticise, though uninformed; themselves unclean, yet demanding a holiness which they, defiled in the dust of the world, felt those in the Temple should sustain for them, and—final provocation—resentful when asked to pay for the cost of that service! The holy prophetic words rose singing in my mind above the profane clamor. "The Lord ye look for shall suddenly come to His Temple." What a place would He find? A shrine? A gateway to the Eternal? Or rather a booth, an open market, a tavern of hucksters at the world's crossways?

As the words rose to my mouth my eye was caught by a group, a group from which angry altercation rose. Alas, the sound of quarreling would not, issuing from that place of the peace of the Lord, have made me pause. What arrested me was a sight. For the angry challenges were rising from a knot of my fellows, men of the Holy Robe, scribes trained to pause before speaking and accustomed to weigh their words while the common people waited on their lips, men of the Strict Observance whose frontlets and headbands, broad and deep with the embroidered words of the Holy Law, spake for them. These men, whose heads carried the awful words, "Hear, O Israel," did not have to strive or cry aloud. They had, where they stood on their own ground, only to intone, "The Lord Is in His Holy Temple," and the masses would reverently repeat, "Let the whole earth keep silence before Him." These were the men now sunk to disputing. "*Who* gives you the right?" "Where's your authority?" "You're an intruder, an impostor." "Why should I give proofs to you?" Spark flashed back to hammer. "You are always challenging. I challenge you!" Yes, I knew the voice, that voice of amazing range, at times as joyously peaceful as the play of sunlight on water, and then flashing with a scorn as blasting as the lightning itself.

I had drawn near and now could see him, hemmed against a pillar and with a ring of authorities around him. Their heads were bent as they watched him. I knew most of them—one or two well. I could read their disturbed minds: their honest distress at these attacks on the Holy Law; their rising irritation at Joshua's open contempt for their office and their service to the Law; their nervous discomfiture that a scene should be made in the Holy Place by an outsider and that they should be discredited in the eyes of strangers by a stranger. It was clear already that he had no fear of them, still less any respect for them. They had lost any initiative or authority which their rank and position might have bestowed. They were together in the arena and a moment more revealed who was the better gladiator.

"You, who are so honestly anxious to search out sanctions, to obey only the most unambiguous authority, who have to know that God has definitely authorized every point of doctrine before you can permit it to be preached to the hungry masses: here is a question for you! The Nazarite Yohannan, was his water purification a lawful rite delegated to him by God because he was a true prophet of the Most High, or was it just a fanatic's fancy?"

Already, behind the ring of cross-questioners a crowd of common people had gathered. Naturally delighted to see the august oracle utterers answered back, this audience had begun to hum with pleasure at such a thrust. The question was a shrewd one; almost everyone outside the hierarchy had now decided that this Nazarite was a prophet, especially since Herod had killed him for his plain speaking. Martyrdom is nearly always the shortest path to spiritual reputation, though that is not to say that it is the surest proof of spirituality. I saw my poor discomforted colleagues look behind them at the sound, surprised that their challenger already had support. A moment before they resembled hounds ringing round a stag, as Joshua stood, back to pillar, head thrown high. Now they were only a thin line of elderly unready men, stubborn frightened sheep caught between an angry shepherd and his skirmishing dogs. They looked again behind them, then unhappily at one another, mumbling something I could not hear.

But Joshua's ringing reply showed, not that they had yielded, but that they had been beaten. "You say, you, the true finders of the law, that on this plain point you can't say. And surely you've had time enough to search the scriptures and make up your minds. Certainly you didn't receive the prophet, did you? Very well, as you can't say yes or no, you can't give a plain answer to that simple question, neither will I tell you my authority. You're no judges of a prophet. That you have proved." Suddenly he strode at them and they gave. The ring was broken. The crowd formed a humming alley for him as he swung down the court.

I could not let his case and theirs so go by default. On the hem of the crowd I kept up with him. As I had approached from my chambers by the gate and he was now going toward it, I was able to keep a little ahead of him. As soon as the crowd saw there was going to be no more authority baiting, they dispersed after some new distraction. When he came to the gate itself we were almost side by side and as nearly alone as a couple may be in a shifting multitude. I was determined to win him back to his great power of winning, if I could. Stepping up to him as he mounted the threshold I gave him the salute of a teacher. I would ask him a question which should show his power and authority, his love of the Law, of the Lawgiver and of the Eternal.

"Rabbi," I called. He stopped dead and his keen eyes swung around upon me. Fire and light were in them. When he had scanned me, reading my heart, the light showed clearly. Even a smile of recollection and interest spread up his face and began to open the cleft furrow between his brows. "Rabbi," I asked, "tell me, which is the great commandment? Where rests the keystone of the Law?"

He had wheeled around and a little group had already gathered. He waited a moment, his head slightly on one side. A gleam of quizzical light began to play around his eyes and to soften his whole face.

"Why," he said with gentle humor, so that the others smiled but did not laugh, "why, here's a man of the Law actually asking questions and not answering them. And it's a great question—indeed the greatest—yet everyone has to answer it for himself." And then with a gentle friendliness of equals, of friends pursuing the same quest, he quickly put out his hand upon my shoulder and looking at me with earnest interest as though he felt that my answer mattered, he asked, "Rabbi, how do you construe the Law here? What do you think it is meant to teach us about our supreme duty?"

His touch, the bitter scene just enacted, the melancholy I had felt previously as I looked on our poor People and us their poor shepherds; the peril of that former day when I had feared to see him butchered just outside this gate; the scenes in Galilee, so bright but ending in cloud and storm —all was a train leading up to this moment and a beacon lit in my mind. Standing with his hand on my shoulder, for he was a step above me—as I was a few steps above the crowd—the words spoke themselves through me. I lifted my head, the sacred summons of the Torah rang out. The crowd turned white with answering faces, white as a lake under the sweep of the tempest, still as the salt beaches of the Dead Sea. "Hear, O Israel, the Lord Thy God is One God and Thou shalt love the Lord Thy God with all thy heart, with all thy mind, with all thy soul and with all thy strength."

I paused, and suddenly I felt with all the conviction of an inspiration that if only we would so love, surely we must cease to bicker and to balk, to wrangle and to cheat. How could we then do other than love our brethren, being all children of such a Father? "And thou shalt love thy neighbor as thyself." The voice that had spoken through me I could hear ringing back, across the struck silence, from the high wall of the Holy of Holies resounding as a confirming word. The hand on my shoulder turned me around. We were through the gate before the crowd moved. "That is it," he said, "on those two principles you, the Law, and we, the prophets, find our common dependence and our single authority. Go on, you are close to the Kingdom where the Father reigns and rules with no harder law than that."

He was gone down the steps vanishing into the street crowd. I passed up the narrow stair to my chambers.

Chapter VII

I *WENT* slowly up the newel stair. The sudden tide of conviction had ebbed. The great words seemed now like noble cloud masses, smitten by the sunlight and riding with quiet majesty over the murk of a malarious plain, which remains in darkness and the shadow of death, a swamp unaffected by the glory that floats above it.

I sat down by the window. Why must prophet and priest, the Law and the Spirit be in conflict! I knew the high moment in which Joshua and I had met could not last. My side would not permit it and he on his side would not brook their rights. He must be persuaded to leave. I would send one of my servants out to the village of Bethany where he was lodged and beg him in the name of the love of God to return north, or, if he would not go to his home, then to the desert. The sense of urgency was on me. I rose to go to the door that I might send my messenger without another moment's delay. As I reached the threshold I heard a foot on the stair. I drew back the door, and facing me was Saul.

"Send Joab to me," I told him.

His answer was a challenge. "Master, I know your purposes. I, who am the servant of your teaching, will save you from this folly. Because I am the child of your mind I know what you plan. Already you have risked compromising your authority. When the Galilean had baited your colleagues, for you openly to take stand with him as he left the Temple was a gratuitous rashness. You shall go no further."

I saw the real devotion under my pupil's passion to dominate. "Why should I not have won his confidence?" I asked. "Surely, now I can send to him as a friend, telling him that he has made his protest, that he has now seen the problem and that the time is now come for him to consider what further steps he should take. I shall propose that he go down to the Essenes by the Dead Sea, who I have been told are his friends, or go west into the desert itself. There he may seek God's will and see how actual conditions may best be helped by his vision." Saul was silent and I thought I had won his assent. "Caiaphas," I added, "is not a vindictive man. We know he does not want trouble now. Even if he thought punishment was meet, he would rather desist and show leniency. No man burdened with keeping to the last moment a vanishing peace, would choose to move against one whom the populace—especially the hotheaded Galileans now packing the city—may at any moment declare a prophet, if not Messiah himself."

Those last words, however, so stung Saul that he broke in. "Safety or no safety, if this hedge prophet claims the mystic kingship he must die. And what's more, you know as well as I do, the Romans will do the job for us if we can prove that he makes the claim. They have warned the next time a fanatic fellow declares he is king of the Jews there will be no time to see whether he can stir up a following. Up on the gallows he goes and those who want to follow can follow him there."

"Then let us urge Joshua to go away!" I suggested.

Saul suddenly became reasonable. "Master, if you urge him to go—you know that kind of hothead—he'll stay. He'll start thinking that he's winning over the Temple and that you and others like you feel his call so strongly that you dare not expose yourself or your colleagues to his fervor and appeal. If you stay quietly aloof, he may tire. . . ."

This was such a change from the fire-breathing denunciation that I on my side began to wonder whether Saul too had begun to experience the prophet's strange charm. True it is, that the surest way to make a man, who is bent on a desperate venture, go still farther is to implore him to save his life before it is too late. Perhaps after all I should be serving his safety best by waiting. Twice he had adventured and each time he had been saved from a final issue by an accident, a mysterious coincidence, but which to a godly man, such as he, must suggest the possibility of divine intervention. I saw Saul's growing relief as I turned the matter over in my mind. I could not but be touched, knowing his personal devotion to me. His was a possessive love, a devotion that would control even its master. But he was caring for my safety and what he said might best serve Joshua's.

"It's only a couple of days now till the Passover," he went on urging, "and then it will be over. After that, with the Galileans gone home, even if he does make a scene or two, Caiaphas will simply hustle him off."

I consented to wait. But the next day proved how mistaken, how misled, I had been. Saul no doubt loved me. But that very love made him additionally dangerous to anyone whom I might respect and whose fortunes my pupil might imagine could involve and endanger my own. I went down into the Temple as usual to attend to my duties. As I passed across the courts, the usual Passover preparation confusion was reaching an even higher pitch than yesterday. When I returned I saw, however, that it had now become an unusual type of turmoil. A tumult centered down near the main gates. I paused to catch the drift of it. An old colleague Eliezar hobbled up to me.

"Well, the authorities are moving at last. Caiaphas seems slow. I'm an impatient man—always was. But I'll own the chief has done it neatly."

"What do you mean?"

"That half-breed is so clever with his tongue that, if you're not ready, he catches you and tosses you back into the howling crowd. But just because he is so quick, he is going to get caught. We have our bait ready and he'll swallow it like a greedy fish. Then we'll land him. Come along and see."

Approaching where the crowd was densest, down by the currency exchange booths and the cattle and pigeon pens, I saw several other scribes converging and Eliezar gave them some lively nods. We stopped on the crowd's rim. But the others pushed their way through until they were close to where the figure of Joshua, standing, I suppose, on the base of a pillar, rose, head and shoulders above the shaggy heads of the swarm of Galileans. He had been, I gathered, preaching to them. But as soon as he saw these other figures he turned on them.

"Here's another story," he called. "An owner had a fine piece of vineyard property. As he was busy with other things, he left agents to manage it. But they were scamps, so they did just as they liked; they let it go to rack and ruin and put what immediate gains could be made into their own pockets. The owner was no fool, however, but a person who thought in long terms and generously. So he sent to them time and again men from his head office to look into their management and put it straight. This simply made the men on the spot certain he was a weak or careless owner. They told his messengers to mind their own business and when the messengers insisted, saying that the owner really couldn't let matters go on like this, the men on the spot beat up the interferers. Some got away badly knocked about. Some were killed. Still the owner didn't come down on them. He said, 'They despise servants like themselves. That's why they don't obey orders from headquarters. Well, then I'll send my son; they can't but respect him.'" At that a queer tenseness ran through all of us. I hardly heard the story end, it was so clear to what conclusion it pointed and what that conclusion must entail. The son also would be killed and that would be the last straw. There could be no doubt about it, Joshua was determined to push his claim to the limit.

I thought that the Pharisees in the front row would now break back, go straight to Caiaphas and attempt with the Temple guards to make an arrest. They had ample evidence; if not evidence on which a court would convict for blasphemy and treason, proof enough for taking into custody. Perhaps, after all, that would be the least of the perils which now seemed to hem around the prophet who was determined to be more than a prophet, or to perish tempting God to save him and to validate his claim. But before I could settle my mind on the issue, I saw another turn had taken place in the rapid tide of events. Was he again to be saved from his desperate determination to die or to dominate? The Pharisees were actually asking him something and he was listening. The crowd was as still as ripe wheat before a thunderstorm while the knot of men around the pillar debated. One had stepped forward as spokesman.

"You know, my good man, we don't deal much in fairy stories here. Pretty enough in the fields, up in the countryside. But, unfortunately, we have to be practical. We are right up against real, pressing, immediate problems. You and these fine fellows of yours, you've come up here expecting to find that we are keeping free worship open for you, the right to worship God as He should be worshipped. You look to us to preserve for you that essential freedom. And we are preserving it. Another Passover, praise be the Lord, is with us and once again, in spite of our being between the nether stone of the army of occupation and the upper stone of your high demands for freedom, we've kept the sacred place open, the sacrifices performed and the Law observed. But the cost is high, very high. High I mean in just what you straightforward, frank men understand to be the hardest to bear, hardest to pay. Now, your man Joshua here, who has given us so many home truths, mixed no doubt with a good deal of shrewd fun, now he will help us out with some honest advice." The speaker had caught his audience. They gaped, while he suddenly swung around on Joshua looking up at him as a lawyer looks when he has a witness cornered. "Quick now: Are we to pay the Roman tribute?"

The stab was cruelly effective. This one question could ruin his prestige or send him straight to the Roman courts. It seemed a fork on one or the other of whose prongs he must be impaled.

Joshua's face did not lose color. On the contrary, it darkened perceptibly. He called out, "Get me a coin." Half a dozen were held out. He snatched one and thrust it under the nose of his prosecutor. "Look at it!" he called. "You can see: you can read. Whose face is it? What's written on it? Answer me!"

I heard the voice of the accuser now actually faltering as he read out, "Tiberius Caesar Imperator Pontifex Maximus."

"The coin then is his, is it not? And what's more, none of you refuse to use it, do you? I haven't seen any of you models of piety throwing these heathen objects away?

Indeed just over there at the money exchange, you're making—some of you—fat fortunes by selling your Temple shekels. You make poor men buy them. And in exchange for your holy silver, branded with pious marks, you accept these very coins reeking of idolatry and emphasizing that you have willingly, and very profitably accepted Caesar's terms. Then have the courage of your contemptible greed. Don't add hypocrisy to avarice. Return to Caesar what he provides for you to use. Pay for the valuable services he yields you. But don't think you can trick me by confusing the issue. Don't try to disguise that your sharp exchange practices are robbing God and His People. Instead of trying to put us off the scent, see that you render Him his due. I warn you, don't try to cover your pious frauds by putting us off the scent with the Roman as a false clue to where the real issue lies.

The crowd of yesterday was there but it was not only larger, it was rougher. Yesterday the spectators had been rude but cheerful, watching a man of themselves sparring with the solemn, pompous, disconcerted authorities and giving better than he got. Today the authorities had blundered far worse. Of course the trap had seemed clever, but now that it was they who were caught in it, it was painfully obvious that they should never have touched it. For the tables could be turned on them. To dispute about the Nazarite Yohannan, dead and forgotten by most, to ask if he had or had not the right to give a water absolution was academic beside the raw issue which these clever fools, in their wish to dig a grave for their enemy, had laid wide open.

There had long been trouble over the rules that compelled men to buy at the Temple's fixed rate of exchange the sacred silver shekel and forbade them to pay their dues in the current coin because it bore on it idolatrous symbols. There was continual wrangling over the regulation that as the sacrificial beasts according to the Law must be without blemish a man could not bring his own animal. If he did bring his own animal the inspectors could usually find some small scar or mark upon it and would insist that he buy one of the certified stock. There was constant scandal about the huge profits that certain Temple families had been making for many years out of this dubious traffic. At Passover times disputes always simmered and seethed to the boiling point of riot. So, it was almost madness to give an opening to an opponent which would permit him to evade the snare, through emphasizing this flagrant grievance. Had Joshua been less hounded he, too, might have seen the danger to the place he loved and with a soft answer have turned away wrath. At least He might have acted on the other Scriptural advice, "Answer not a fool according to his folly." But he had, it was clear, been stung to the quick. He had been traduced and these men had tried to lure him to his destruction. It stung him to feel that his enemies would stoop to anything, would call black white to get him soiled with the pitch.

When he had finished speaking, the crowd did not laugh: it growled. I have noticed that crowds, when they shout, may easily be deflected, but when the note becomes low then riot is always near. All eyes were upon him. They were watching whether he would give a signal. They would wait until he moved and when he moved he would be letting loose a torrent of dammed up resentment. We all waited, looking at him. We saw his eye travel around those wary watching faces of officialdom, blanching with apprehension as they realized their peril. His voice sounded low, but terribly clear, not only because of the strained hush but because of the cold intensity with which he spoke.

"You, the guardians of God's Law and of His Sanctuary,

listen to His Law. Deny it if you will—'My house shall be called a house of prayer.' A house of prayer! A den of beasts of prey, a robber's cave, is what you have made it."

And at that instant, from one of the exchange tables broke out a howling protest. In broad Galilean a peasant was protesting that here in God's House he was being cheated by being handed false change. His fellows turned shouting sympathy. The beadle tried with his staff to beat back the man who was attempting to snatch the coins of which he thought he had been defrauded. Like an angry hive all the Galileans around, and many scattered about in the vast court, bore down on the struggling group. Then in a flash Joshua was through them. How much of the warrior Messiah was in the man who wanted only to be the peaceful Priest-King. He took command at once. The crowd ranged behind its natural leader. To his abrupt "stand aside" the poor beadle only made a feeble flourish of his staff. Joshua brushed it aside like a wisp of straw. Then he turned suddenly, seized the edge of the table with its drawers of money, its little wells of coin, its heaps of tallies and checkers. Up it went and crashed over on the wretched little huckster crouching behind it. The crowd roared. Over went another table. The money ran cascading in every direction. The crowd joined in. Here was the chance at last to pay back many an old and sharp score. The heaped up crates and cages of the doves came next. They tore to splinters and the birds flew out whirling and flapping. The stools their sellers sat upon were whisked from under them. Men sprawled in every direction. Now the cattle stalls were reached. Joshua had picked up a kind of besom made of cords plaited to a short broom handle—a thing with which the herdsmen used to sweep out their area. Swinging this over his head, he trounced the cattle till they broke from their pens. Like a tide, the Galileans cheering in the rear, the oxen stampeding ahead, the frightened birds wheeling and swooping above, Joshua in the midst, ran the bellowing shouting concourse towards the main gates. Seeing the panic-struck cattle with their heads down making for the gates, the doorkeepers fled. Even the two soldiers on duty drew into the sentry cells on either side. The wild medley poured out into the streets beyond.

I turned back to the almost empty court. The small group of scribes who by their shallow cunning had lit this mine of resentment, were already hurrying off. They were going, I felt sure, to report the result of their ruse to headquarters. However much they were to blame, however much this grotesque miscarriage of their plan was wholly their fault, such a riot would not and could not be forgiven. Many of the men whose stock had been dispersed and whose capital lost—I had seen many a hand stoop down and pick the scattered coin as it lay thick upon the pavement—were small people who paid highly for their posts and had to work hard to make their profits. The big men behind who drew the big royalties, they were untouched. They would find plenty more agents to whom they could farm these sources of revenue. Still, however, I had hope that Joshua would see now that his protests had miscarried. For the third time he had been saved from the consequences of his intervention. The camel caravan had turned his small pageant back. He had acted out that part he had either planned or which had come upon him; he had lived out the parable of how the peaceful Messiah should enter on his rule, and when people had seen, and before authority could strike, he was carried into safety. He had next challenged the teachers themselves in the Temple, and had been enabled to show that though the scribes might cavil at the prophet's credentials, there was a common foundation of loyalty binding them together—the Law and the two great commandments.

Finally, he had put his protest into action. Surely he could hope now that the priesthood and the men of the Law would be awakened to the bitter discontent their all too easy and too gainful practice of religion had caused among those on whose support they lived? He had shown that their protest against Rome was an overlooking of a grievance which they themselves could right and must right if ever they were to have behind them a loyal people in their demand to live only, wholly and directly under God. And now that he, the peaceful Messiah, had become the man of direct action, and of forcible eviction, his defiance risking arrest and punishment, even here the Guider of all events had a third time let him be swept by his own outburst into safety. I could only see a divine, a fatherly providence in this, and I felt convinced it was so manifest that he himself must see it too.

Shaken, then, though I was by these events I went to my chamber, as one who has seen a tempest go over his land breaking down ill-rooted trees but leaving the well-planted standing. Tomorrow we could tend to the salvage and learn by our lesson. I felt a great weariness as though the crisis had come and, reaching its final expression, had passed. As soon as the light failed I went to my bedchamber. In any case the next night must keep me up late for then the Temple would begin the celebration of the Passover.

However, as might be expected, I slept poorly. The scenes of the last few days followed me in fantastic forms into my broken dreams. So I hardly knew whether it was a dream of yesterday or a present fact when I saw lights moving on the ceiling of my room and heard urgent but muted voices rising from below. I raised my head, knowing I was fully awake and, as instantly, that some urgent process was afoot, some fresh scene of tragedy unfolding. But when I reached my window, which looked out over the main court of the Temple, I was only in time to see the end of a small torchlit procession disappearing around a bastion in the direction of the main administrative buildings. The authorities, without consulting us, the jurists, had been undertaking some action they felt it best to carry out while the populace was asleep. I could never remember having witnessed such a procedure. Yet there came into my mind another question: could I remember an occasion when their rule had been so persistently and successfully challenged at the very center of their power? The two thoughts converging left me no longer in doubt. They had succeeded in arresting Joshua. Sleep now was gone for the night. But action also was useless. Caiphas and his executive committee of the Sanhedrin had every right to lay hold of Joshua if they could, to interrogate him as to his intentions, to try to obtain from him a promise to cease molesting them at their functions. They had every right to bind him over to keep the peace, even if he could not obtain surety for the losses he had inflicted on men who at worst were only agents in a long-established traffic.

Still, though I had no legal right to be present and no moral right to intervene in a civil action of this sort, I could not stay still in my chamber, ignorant of what was taking place within a furlong of me. There was then in the Temple a gallery which ran from the chambers occupied by us the jurists, near and over the gates, right along the upper part of the side wall. This permitted us to reach the archives and the executive buildings without having to go down and cross the main court. This gallery was a timber construction hanging out high above ground level and, as it ran on the outside of the main wall near its top, I would often when I slept ill, walk up and down its length looking out over the sleeping city that lay spreading beneath. I put on a cloak and let myself out into this high passage. Where it bent at right angles, I could see down its full length, which was the length of the greater part of the Temple itself. Almost at its end, a beam of light shone across the darkness. I knew what that meant. In the daytime certain of the executive chambers at that end obtained part of their lighting from high windows outside which this gallery ran. I went at once toward the light. My conjecture had been correct: standing by the deep embrasure, so that I was invisible to those within and below, I could see at a glance that I was overlooking the whole room which lay twenty feet below me. This was the chamber in which the executive committee of the Sanhedrin always met.

Caiaphas was already in his seat of office. Surely he had been waiting. A full quorum of his colleagues was present in their robes. The court officials necessary for a trial were also mustered in their uniforms. Armed guards were at their stations. In one corner stood a small shabby group: those were, I knew, witnesses held in reserve. Yes, authority was striking back. And in the midst on the spot where the prisoner is set to face the court and to confront his accusers, stood Joshua. The place was fully lit and I could look straight across at his face which was tilted so that, though he was facing Caiaphas and the court, his eyes were looking out over their heads. Caiaphas was vibrant with anxiety, calling the court to order again and again. The other members were equally restless. The latent disturbance came to a head when Zadok, the eldest member, rose. I'd known him many years. Very old now, he had been a great lawyer and I had often sought his profound statute knowledge.

"I rise to a point of competence. To this court are delegated powers by the Sanhedrin, specific powers of executive administration. I stand to ask, do powers delegated cover extemporized trials for blasphemy and treason? I move that this matter be referred back for legality to the original authorizing power."

I knew the old man's legal knowledge. So did Caiaphas. His powerful hands twisted the linen ephod which he wore as presiding magistrate until it began to tear. There was little doubt that the high priest was straining the instructions and delegation that had been given him, and myself, as a lawyer, knew that in a case of procedure Zadok's challenge for a stay of process should be sustained. Caiaphas, however, was quick as a cornered man can be. If he waited, he was now certain, all was lost. The Galileans would learn that their champion had been seized. They were quite fearless. They would flock to Pilate and demand the customary Passover boon, the release of a prisoner and, past doubt, he would grant it. Quite likely even now he had never heard Joshua's name and when he saw him, as he was a shrewd judge of men, he would size him up as far more likely to vex the priesthood, whom Pilate scorned and liked to have discredited, than to constitute a danger to the Imperial forces.

Caiaphas turned on the legalists. "Do you want the whole people massacred while you carry on discussions whether you have the power to put out of the way one troublemaker?" Then, swinging around on Joshua, he poured forth a series of interrogations. But to all of this the prisoner paid not the slightest attention. Neither the wrangle that might have set him free nor the thrusts of the judge who had become the prosecutor and who was trying to extract from him a damning confession seemed to enter his ears. He continued to gaze fixedly at the wall over Caiaphas' head.

"Answer! Answer!" shouted the angry priest, and one of the guards taking his cue from such behavior suddenly joined in, "You dare to refuse. Answer to his Honor!" And with that he struck Joshua full on the mouth.

The prisoner turned as quietly as one whose shoulder has been touched by an inquirer and said as unconcernedly, "If I've made a mistake, point it out. Otherwise why hit me?"

That calm reply checked the unseemly excitement and Caiaphas, trying to recollect himself, called, "Bring the witnesses forward."

But this, too, was mismanaged. Zadok was upon his feet again. "The Holy Law requires always that there be two witnesses in tested concurrence on each point."

Caiaphas had to submit. Zadok (how well an old lawyer will keep his mastery of procedure) took their stories quickly and in a few cross questions exposed flagrant contradictions. No doubt they had heard Joshua make some strange and possibly exaggerated remarks. That he was both a poet of wonderful imagery and a prophet of righteous angers, I well knew. But they could give no definite statements which could endure a competent cross-examination.

"No case," said Zadok wearily turning to the chair and sitting down.

Caiaphas was now clearly desperate. There ensued one of those strange pauses when time seems to stop. The court had become completely silent. Joshua's calm was so great that he seemed almost to have passed into a trance. The committee, it was now plain, would not move. They sat stonily watching Caiaphas, for though he was a powerful man he was certainly not one that was loved. He himself looked as though he were at his wits' end, he the cornered man and not the prisoner. Then from the end of the courtroom beyond my view, came the sound of some half-muffled dispute. It roused Caiaphas for a moment and he shook his hand with impatience in that direction at this small disturbance. But, stranger, it roused Joshua too. For the first time he lowered his eyes, not to look at the court but to look, also, towards the door out of my sight. I heard a door close, and the silence as it settled again was so complete that behind me somewhere out in the city I heard a cock crow. I turned to look behind me. Already far over the Moab country the sky was turning that ashen tint which marks the death of night rather than the birth of day. On looking back into the hall nothing had changed, but Caiaphas was now staring at his prisoner as though at last the moment had come when one or the other must perish. But Joshua's eyes were again lifted and were gazing with unwavering intensity at the empty wall. Suddenly the chief priest raised his arms and with a cry which blended fear and anger in a terrible intensity, he shouted, "I charge you in the name of the living God, say who you are. Are you the Messiah, the Son of the Blessed?"

Even old Zadok drew back in his seat at such wild procedure. Now Joshua would speak: would explain his prophetic message and must be let go. I knew the feeling of the court and I knew that it could and would now insist on that elementary equity. Joshua had won his right to liberty through Caiaphas' obvious mismanagement and blind determination to wrest the Law to his wishes. The prisoner, who time and again had proved himself to be so able a debater on difficult points, would certainly not play into such a clumsy trickster's hands but, as he had always done before, exploit to the utmost the advantage given him by the uncontrolled animus of his enemies. He lowered his eyes. Even if he kept silent the court would now sustain him. But he was going to speak. As quietly as he had asked why he had been struck for holding his peace, he answered to this preposterous question, "Yes."

I thought the silence that lay over the court could not

have deepened. But it did. Men stood and sat like stone. Caiaphas moved not a muscle.

"Yes, I am," went on the voice, "and every one of you will soon see me descending on clouds of glory from God's right hand to judge you and the whole earth."

Caiaphas recovered first. He turned to Zadok. "You won't be needing any more witnesses now, will you?" His voice was almost choked with the terrible relief. "You have heard what's just been said?" Then, his voice arose almost to a shriek, "Blasphemy." He tore the ephod from his shoulders, ripping it to shreds and threw the tatters on the ground. Then he looked around on his colleagues. Silently they all bowed their heads. Now, however, he was alive again. In a moment he had called the four nearest him; close friends—if there is any friendship at the top—close friends, at least now that he was winning. I could hear his quick commanding voice. "Dawn is near. You must come with me at once to Pilate. He'll take our joint witness. If he hesitates I'll tell him how it will sound in Rome when Caesar learns that he let a usurper go. Maybe we can't any longer execute blasphemers but we can yet work the engine which does execute. Before the city is up we'll have Pilate's signature on the death warrant. There will be no attempt at rescue when once the legions are known to be standing to arms. What's more, we know that men care only for success. Once the People see this felon in the hands of the execution squad, mark my words they'll only be wanting to see him hanged."

He gave them these instructions, shepherding them on all the while. He was now completely at his ease. He had won. Joshua, in his mind, was already dead. Human beings never really meant anything to Caiaphas. They made a mass that had to be molded. When one rose out of the mass he had to be struck back into the lump. Caiaphas only hated when he feared he was failing. Indeed, he went out past Joshua without seeming to notice him and Joshua did not turn his head either. The remainder of the colleagues, old and weary, dispersed to get what sleep they might, for tomorrow would be for them a long day of extensive ceremonies. The ushers began to quench the lamps, and then, with authority gone, Caiaphas' grim words fulfilled themselves. The guards turned on Joshua who yet stood steadily gazing into the distance as though he were watching something to us invisible but approaching. With the malicious cruelty which our justice seems to rouse in those to whom we leave its execution, they began to strike at the lonely figure. This was intolerable. The Holy Law is perhaps a stone which, if it shall fall upon a man, it shall grind him to powder but those who suffer its penalties are not to be exposed to tormenting mockery. My heart rose in me that in the Temple and before my eyes I, who could speak from the seat of the Law, should see such shameful manhandling take place. Should we who taught mercy as the message of the All Merciful, permit one, however terribly mistaken, to be tormented? One who had healed the sick and taken pity upon the insane? Was he not because of a desperate courage facing with patient resignation a doom terrible enough to awaken compassion? I could not reach the room below by going further along the passage down into the archive room which led to the judgment chamber because that door at night was locked. I must hasten back whence I had come, go down by the gate stair, cross the main court and put a stop to this brutality.

I hurried. But when I arrived the hall had emptied and it was already dusk. To my demand, where is the prisoner? a sleepy usher told me that Caiaphas had sent back for him and he had been led away. I went down to the door which led out through the side wall of the Temple. But the street was vacant in the pale dawn. I stood hesitating and then in the stillness heard by the side of the steps which led to street level and on the top of which I was standing, a moaning. In the shadow of the corner a man was crouched, his shoulders heaving. My own misery sent me to him. He turned at my touch and in the pale light I saw a rough face, grey and distorted by grief, grief so great that, though obviously he was a peasant, all fear of an official was banished, all sense of me as a stranger was gone. With the harsh sobs which make a grown man's crying almost a physical pain, in the thick Galilean burr, he gasped out,

"They've taken him and here am I a cur, that hasn't even the guts to get kicked out of the way. And he said it. I, with my drunkard's courage, I, the poltroon of the whole pack of rats, when he said,"—the poor fellow howled for a moment like an animal in pain—" 'You'll all run for your lives,' I stated, 'Everyone else will, but you'll see me stand.' And I can hear him, and shall hear him, to my dying day, reply, 'This night, before the cock signals the end of it, you'll actually swear that you don't even know me.' When they took him, sure enough we all ran like hares. Then I came back and crept in here by the door. But someone, suspecting I was a Galilean, challenged me. My panic came back. I saw all was up. I swore I knew nothing. I thought he'd gone blind to us all. But, oh, God help me, right as I swore, I heard outside a cock crow. I looked across at him and he was looking straight at me. I'll never forget those eyes. O my Master, if only you had hated me. I cannot live, for he is going to die. And he does not hate me. But can he ever forgive me, can I ever forgive myself?"

His grief was so intense, the poor toilworn body writhed as though in a death agony. I knelt beside him. Such sorrow melts away all rank. When I was close to him I saw his face.

Where had I seen it before? For a moment the spasm of grief that held it distorted, relaxed and I remembered. This was the fisherman who had given me the first description of Joshua when I first entered Galilee on my search. How long ago it seemed: how from another world seemed to shine behind this dead and tragic dawn that spring sunshine by the waterside. The body beside me was shaken with the fever of its sorrow. Then the head turned slowly and regarded me for a while with expressionless eyes that gradually focused.

"Who are you? You're one of them, one of them that have killed him!"

I rose and waited.

"Who are you?" His voice was half resentful, half frightened.

"Son," I answered, "we have met before. I came to Galilee last year."

He seemed to recall nothing. "Your lot has sent him to his death."

I had neither wish nor need to defend Caiaphas' procedure. So I asked him, "Do you know that your friend was betrayed into blasphemy . . . ?"

"Betrayed, yes," came the reply, "by that hound Judas."

"No: he betrayed himself."

"Oh, he knew he was betrayed, knew that it was all up. How I begged him not to move unless we were ready to strike. But I'm sure he knew that Judas was going to sell the secret. He made us swear not to tell anyone. It was I who recognized first who he was. But when he knew the secret was sold then he rushed on his fate."

"But he did intend to claim the throne and the Divine Judgeship at some moment?"

The man at my feet rolled round and sat upright. "You want to catch me, too!"

"No: I'm not a judge and I have always sought mercy."

"But you didn't raise a finger to save him!"

I would not enter into our desperate problem with a stranger, so asked him, "Did you?"

This brought on another paroxysm of weeping. Then with a recovery as swift, "But I will do something. I can die with him. Perhaps rescue him."

"He is now in the hands of the Romans. They are harder to deal with than our own masters."

His face worked. Finally he brought out, "You're not our leaders. You betray our leaders. You're on the side of Rome."

At that moment one of the doorkeepers looked out to see what the voices outside signified. Evidently the Galilean thought he had been too rash, that here was a force coming at my beck to seize him. He scrambled to his feet, his pathetic face half defiant, half panic-stricken. He made off down the narrow lane that skirted the outer wall of the Temple. I turned and went heavily to my room.

In the volume of national events how small a ripple the sinking of one soul makes in the general tide. The Passover was celebrated with the usual state, the accustomed sacrifice, the chants, the prayers, the processions and the blessings. Caiaphas stood in his robes and sprinkled the vast masses of people, himself looking as peaceful and assured as though these offices were his only interest and activity, and the people as peaceful and dutiful as though they were the sheltered sheep of a trusted shepherd. The storms of human passion cannot be foreseen nor thwarted but neither can they be sustained. So the Eternal has made us. But the long and bloodstained ritual wearied my spirit, already tired and sad. The great questing words of the Psalms kept chanting in my ears, "Thinkest thou that I will drink Bull's blood. Offer me the sacrifice of righteousness," and the prophet's words answered me. "What does the Lord require of thee but to deal justly, love mercy, and walk humbly with him?" Had we loved mercy? Was that proud vestmented man who was now calling on God's help with such assurance one who had walked humbly? Could these sacrifices avail? However wild Joshua had been, could Caiaphas avoid the blame of having driven him to blasphemy? Could we avoid blood guiltiness in his death?

Chapter VIII

THE DAYS following I passed closeted in study. I had many judgments to give. I had to issue a number of writings, which have now been codified under regulations governing marriage, so that they might be published to those of the Dispersion and serve for their guidance. The discipline of thorough research and setting forth principles in unambiguous and clearly ordered form kept my mind from the fruitless regrets that otherwise would have invaded it. At last Pentecost was come, and I had completed the texts and issued the proclamations before the day the pilgrims would depart and the city relapse into its usual routine. I had gone out to see that the orders were placarded in all the authorized places when on returning to my chambers I found Saul waiting for me. I had not seen him since the Passover. I saw at once he was excited but also that some misgiving was working in him.

"Rabbi," he began at once, "the city is in a disturbed state."

"Isn't it always so with the pilgrims leaving?" I questioned.

"Yes, yes." Then he hesitated. I had often seen Saul so pent with what he had to say that the words congested in his throat. I had never seen him checked by being of two minds. He had sometimes had doubts as to whether he dare say before me what he wished, but never a doubt as to his own conviction. Now he was, I surmised, a house divided against itself. What could have caused this unprecedented change, I kept wondering. He began again. "Rabbi, do you remember those—those disturbances before the Passover?"

I nodded.

"Perhaps you do not know how they were ended?"

"Much can be kept by the Levites," I replied, "from the guardians of the Law. Law and Temple have almost parted asunder. But one who is charged to issue rulings can and must know what the masters of the Temple do, though he cannot intervene if they are within their rights."

"Then you own they were right."

"I can only say that if even a prophet speak on oath before them what the priests consider blasphemy, no master of the Law can intervene to save the speaker. He of whom we are speaking, though he attacked the dubious trading in the Temple, did not denounce those carved and blazoned words he and all of us have read and by our silence approved. Over the gateway to the Inner Holy Place are inscribed the words, 'He who crosses this threshold is the cause of his own death.' Therefore, if he maintained his own words to be free of blasphemy, he must depend wholly on God by manifest sign and witness to validate him. Saul," I said with all my heart going out to both these men, to the one who had striven so passionately and suffered such a passion, and to the other who was suffering and I felt must suffer as much as the former he so shunned, "Saul, is it not always the final temptation of the just to tempt God, to dare Him to intervene on their behalf because He dare not let His cause, which they have deliberately put in hazard, go down in defeat? His appeal was to God and to God we must leave it. Further, should he add to the blasphemy, a violation of the Roman law of treason, then not only must he answer to God, but he must answer to Caesar. And if he is not a Roman citizen his body must bow and be broken under Pilate's sentence."

"Then you know what happened?"

"I cannot see how Pilate dared do otherwise than condemn. The case on the Roman point was clearer even than on the Hebrew."

Saul answered, "Pilate did, I understand, all he could to save him. Evidently he thought the prisoner harmless politically, and, of course, if he could, he would disoblige and discredit the priests. But, as you say, he could not run the risk that they could say this was the liberating Messiah and that Pilate let him get away!"

Then with a sudden change as though a mist of doubtful mercy had vanished from the hot sun of conviction:

"But the Most High has spoken. This wild defiant man has appealed to the Eternal against the decision of the Eternal's Law and Lawful judges and God Himself has given him over to the judgment. As it is written, 'Cursed is he that hangs on the tree!' "

"The Scriptures require searching and weighing. I feel that this man has paid his penalty and I know he paid it with wonderful submission to the Eternal Father's judgment. Was Job utterly abandoned after he submitted to God? Was Jonah left as the prey of Leviathan after he turned in the depth of the sea and confessed his wrong willfullness. What says the prophet of the final justification of the suffering servant?"

I saw again doubt spreading in Saul's mind. But, alas, though he could endure all else, he could never suffer the pain of uncertainty, could never wait upon God in darkness. He started up, "No, no, God has spoken with final judgment."

"That," I said, "might be spoken by a Sadducee but not by our School which holds the Holy Hope. Is death the end of God's Mercy? Do not the Psalms say, 'I will not leave my holy one in the grave'?"

A strange look, more of fear than aught else passed over his dark face. "You don't mean . . . I mean, have you been hearing this . . . this gossip?"

I did not know what he meant and did not wish to excite him more, so only added, "God may permit a man to be judged by his acts in this life. But seeing the heart and the motive, after this life and its costs have been discharged, surely, He will again show the countenance of His Mercy and welcome home a wayward son."

At that Saul darted up, "No, no, either God gives a sign, a sign, or the judgment and the actual execution stand."

"But the man spoke so strongly against the asking for signs."

"Exactly: he knew he dare not risk it."

"But he did in the end risk all."

"And the Most High did decide against him by silence."

"I ask again does that disprove the good he taught? Surely only the mistaken act he made? The teaching is our holy father Hillel's. . . ."

"No, no, either the judgment is revoked—and can that be! *Can that be!* It stands against him a final doom forever. I must go. You do not know, father, what is ahead. These men, too long deluded, are now quite mad. We did not strike soon enough. The contagion is spread. The accursed tree is cut down, but it has seeded. Out in the streets now —and that is why I came to you for encouragement," his voice grew harsh, "and found none—out through the city these crazed fools are saying they must form a new society, that God has told them to, because the man who is dead and buried has come alive and is with them now forever." He had risen to his feet almost in a frenzy, and with last words he turned from the room without farewell and rushed down the stairs.

Chapter IX

As *SAUL'S* footsteps died away I went to a side door and called my servant Joab, a trustworthy and stable man. To my question, was the City quiet now that the pilgrims had departed? he said Yes. When I asked whether he had heard of any excitement he answered that some were saying a group of Galileans had stayed on. It was thought they might be associates of the Nazarene who had caused the brief riot in the Temple just before the Passover and had been arrested and handed over to the Romans before the trouble spread.

"The loss of their leader should have discouraged them," I said.

"It did for a time," he replied. "At least they lay very low when he was being put out of the way and for a month or so after. But now it looks as though they have found another leader—a fisherman."

"None of them showed the stuff of leadership when their prophet was seized, did they?" I asked.

"Peasants can never stand up to the quality," Joab replied with that quiet conviction in authority which loyal servants always display and which gives the masters half their conviction of their own mastery.

"Why, then, with their leader gone are they stirring again?"

My question seemed to make Joab uneasy. His eyes ran to and fro following the pattern of the rug on the floor. "You see, Master," he finally began, "they have among them a number of excitable women. One is quite well known, or, at least, was." He paused again. "You, Master, would never have heard of her. She was a disreputable dancer, came from Magdala. Her family had cast her out. She had a diabolic temper and when she raged an armed man was afraid of her. Her fury would pass, I've been told by those who saw her, into a kind of fit when she would fall foaming. She says the Galilean cured her. She had mocked him and when he was unruffled, she went mad and flew at him. He didn't give a step but took her attack in his open hands. As soon as she touched them she fell at his feet in convulsive weeping. He raised her, she struggling to get away, shouting that he couldn't know what filth he was handling and that his fingers burned her like vinegar in a wound. But he went on saying," Joab paused, "at least that's what I've been told, that the past didn't matter. Her evil had been due to the mistaken way she was trying to find love. And now she had found the true way she would be all right. All she had to do was to believe that and . . ." Again he paused and raised his eyes to me.

I knew why he hesitated and I completed his sentence, "her sins were forgiven."

He nodded silently in assent. "No one can forgive sins but God?" Joab questioned me.

"None," I replied, "but we have been taught that He may send the assurance of His Fatherly forgiveness through the lips of one of His children."

"Well, she then naturally followed him like a dog that's been saved from street urchins. She was utterly fearless, as that sort often is, and tough as nails. She went everywhere with his lot. She never had another attack and, I've been told, when all those hardy countrymen scurried like mice she actually trailed the execution party right up to the mound. After all, she was used to soldiers and their ways.

If you think of it she'd probably be safer with them than a man would. The shock, however, was, naturally enough, too much for her. He was her life. She had lived on the fact that he was alive, that there was one man who could stand up to her and not strike her; and who could love her and not desire her. He really cared for her and she had no power over him. He could do everything for her—give her back sanity, health, happiness, and she could do nothing for him. She wouldn't, just couldn't believe he was dead. They say she went and sat in the graveyard where Pilate had let the body be put away, the greater part of the night and almost before daybreak rushed into the hide-out of the Galileans and," he paused, then went on in some confusion, "and said she'd seen him alive, that he'd spoken to her. He said that everything had gone right: that he had succeeded far beyond their dreams: that he had to die to get through." He stopped. "Sir, I am afraid I'm not making it at all clear but then it's a complete muddle to me. But that's what they are all saying. It's a queer story for a heartbroken harlot to make up, isn't it?"

I allowed that it was, and asked him if there were more to tell.

"Only, sir, that, as I have heard often happens, when a wild woman begins seeing things then the rest who otherwise never would, begin to see things too. They were all saying they saw him, here, there, all over the place. But she said he'd told her they were to go back to Galilee and he'd meet them there, a far cry from the tomb here. I'm told the men suddenly were against that and said they were told to stay here. The men won, though I'm not sure a few didn't go up to the lake just to see. The end of the story is that yesterday morning they ran into the north market place from their hide-out, those men who'd been skulking like half drowned rats, and made such a din that business stopped while they harangued the crowd. I'm told no one knew quite what they were saying, but their excitement, their wild joy was so catching that the crowd caught it too. Someone said they were drunk. But their leader said, not at all: that it was too early in the day to be tipsy. It was just joy, he said, because they had found out that everything was all right, that their master was alive and that death didn't really exist."

"I wonder," I said, "whether it will last: I wonder whether they will feel that way when they, like him, are facing death. He was brave, very brave and calm but he was not exultant."

I found the report of Joab invaluable later. For some ten days hence I had to decide on action. I noticed some of the Galileans in the Temple again. They were, however, quietly behaved. Some of them spent most of their time in prayer. I observed also on their faces a cheerfulness which is rare on the faces of men who toil as hard as these fishermen toil and have as little to look forward to. Then one day one of the ushers came up to me and said that a man was behaving strangely, that he had been asked to be quiet and had refused.

"He's in a sort of religious ecstasy, Sir, and not perhaps to blame because he's thanking God for giving him back his legs. He's a well-known Temple beggar and I testify he's not been able to walk since childhood and he's forty now if he's a day."

"Well," I remarked as we went over to the place where a small procession was forming in the arcade called Solomon's Porch, "perhaps if we had been motionless for that time we might caper with thankfulness when set free." True enough there was a man in rags skipping about and at his side were two Galileans.

"They cured me," the man kept crying. "This man," and

he pointed to the Galilean nearest to us, "this man simply said 'Look into my eyes.' I did and he said, 'In the name of Joshua of Nazareth get up.' He pulled me up and I found I could stand. What's more, I felt my legs spring up under me." And he hopped again into the air.

But what really surprised me was that the man he called the thaumaturge was none other than the poor broken fellow I'd spoken to that Passover Eve after the night trial, none other than the simple fisherman of Galilee. The change in him was more remarkable than the beggar's recovery. He strode along as master of the place. Already a trail of those pathetic and helpless creatures that always hang around the Temple porches asking alms and advertising their needs by the evidence of their diseases and mutilations, was following the small group of three. And already the fisherman was taking the lead shouting out, "Give praise to God. Look at the man healed by our Lord Joshua." I hoped that after a short parade they would leave. But they went on their noisy way till up by the Levites' quarters the door guards came out with their staves and ordered them to cease disturbing the peace and to be gone. I heard the leader say, "No, no, we must not be silent about God's power. He raised up our Lord Joshua after your people had killed him and now we're bringing you proof. This man is on his legs again, through the power of our Joshua." At this the cured beggar began again to shout and caper and so did the tatterdemalion crowd. The guards were evidently becoming nervous. Suddenly making a grab, they caught the two Galileans and dragged them within the court gate, drove back the rest of the crowd with a flourish of their staves, and then slammed the doors in their faces. The crowd, left without its leaders, soon dispersed. The Galileans did not return.

I was told later that the executive committee sat on the

case the next day. They certainly wanted no more trouble but the matter was particularly provoking to them. My servant Joab had been an accurate reporter. The renewal of the disturbance had turned on the Galileans' insisting, not that they were healing people by the power of God—or they were claiming miraculous cures right and left—but that this power was transmitted to them through a dead man. No one who studies and practices prayer but may know that God's arm is not shortened; as He did through the prophets so He will do this day if He is given faith. The Canon may close, but the voice of God, though it has spoken in the Law forever, still illustrates by acts of mercy that covenant of mercy which joins Him and all who trust in Him. The priesthood cannot, and would not, deny miracles lest they deny the sign of God's finger. We of the Law and they of the sacrifice have a right and duty to demand proof of authenticity. But none of us has the right to put it aside, if to the sign is added the witness of humility and purity of life and the acknowledgment of the Law as God's basic revelation. We of the Law, we Pharisees who hold the Scriptures imply the Life Eternal, we have no issue—on the contrary, a close agreement—with those who maintain the resurrection of the dead at the Last Day. What we hold is that, till then, the blessed departed sleep in God and all that men see when the spirit has left the body is the wraith of the passion, an echo of its cry for justification. The Sadducees who wholly control the Temple and the priesthood say, however, that any survival is denied by the Law and is a foreign superstition. The Galileans were then not only alarming the executive council by declaring a convicted man had been justified by God, but the proof which they adduced for this offensive claim was itself of all possible proofs most provocative.

I was then surprised at their leniency; for Joab told me

that evening that the two men were at large again and, as always happens when a defiance of authority proves successful, the enthusiasm in their group mounted to exultation.

The stories now told of them assumed a sinister tinge as the power they felt went to their leaders' heads. They had set up a loosely organized commune for all who joined them, and their few prosperous members paid in their resources to keep this relief scheme going. The Galilean fisherman had made himself the head. As a rule this impulsive type that boasts before action and turns tail under fire, fulfills his promises upon attaining success, and wipes out his disgrace by seizing the initiative and asserting himself. It was said that he had established his ascendancy by methods more befitting a magician than the penitent renegade of a master of mercy. When crowd excitement is high morbid seizures are common, and I have noticed when healers are practising, some patients are made far worse when others are recovering. The story that Joab brought me was, however, an ill one, whatever the actual explanation. A man had sold some land for the new cause and brought the money to the leader. But the leader, suspecting that not all money received was being paid in, questioned the donor, who declared he was giving every penny. At this the leader flew into a passion, denounced the donor as a cheater of God and the man collapsed. Shortly after, his wife, not knowing of his lie and his death, appeared. She was similarly cross-questioned, also lied and was similarly denounced and fell dead.

Painful as these events would be to any compassionate man, they gave the impulsive peasant a sense of power and a conviction that he could challenge again the authorities. He came with a large crowd once more into the arcades of Solomon's Porch in the Temple. After he had prayed, he proceeded to preach to them again on the execution of

Joshua and how he was now alive, inspiring the acts of these Galileans who were to be in the future his fully accredited representatives. Naturally, as soon as this was reported to the authorities they dispatched an adequate force of constables. The fisherman leader certainly then showed no miraculous power. His followers quietly let him and his young companion be taken. What then happened is difficult to determine. They were locked up, but appear to have escaped. Their release, they claimed, was another miracle, and to prove their point they regathered their crowd in the Solomon Porch. Again the authorities seized them. It was at this point that I was summoned. As I was only that year become forty this was one of my first Sanhedrin sessions, my election not being but a month past. I realized how confused the executive committee must have been to summon a full meeting of the council. A number of them had only consented to that fatal trial for blasphemy because of Caiaphas' argument. He had urged at the Passovertide that the political situation was critical, that if a disturber, who had the people behind him and was blasphemously claiming divine power, was not removed, then the Romans would be massacring the entire populace. And now with the Feast over and the disturber dead here was the same problem recurring.

When I arrived in the chamber, the court was only waiting the call to order. The two Galileans stood before the dais. The older one I now would hardly have recognized. Obviously he felt himself no longer an equal of the court but as its superior. His companion was much younger, with a gentle and beautiful face, still the face of a boy.

Old Annas had again sufficiently recovered to preside. He was very old but age had not made him lenient. He opened the proceedings quietly enough. Sternly, but without show of anger, he asked the prisoners what they meant by flatly disobeying the court's injunction. The elder replied coolly that they had no intention of obeying the authorities if such orders were contrary to those given to them by God. Old men in office seldom can stand being treated disrespectfully. The veins on the forehead of the old man stood out and, heaving himself from his chair, he shouted at them.

"You're to judge," replied the fisherman, "the only point at issue is whether one is to obey men like you or God Himself!"

Annas was beside himself at such insolence. He whirled around to the court. "You see," he gasped, "no other action is possible: they must be executed too."

There was dissent at this. No capital crime had been committed—at least if we omit their private boast of having killed two of their own subscribers. A good deal of confused comment resulted, while the elder Galilean looked on with open contempt and both of them seemed quite indifferent to their fate. As I watched them the history of the last year ran through my mind. The whole was epitomized in that rugged face now set in a stolid calm. The features had not changed. This was still the kindly puzzled peasant, woken in middle life to the fact that a local carpenter's son had miraculous powers, that (disconcerting but inescapable fact) the words which he had listened to every Sabbath all his life with conventional assent, had suddenly been fulfilled in the local village. This was the hard-working family man suddenly having to forsake work and family. This was the simple man who had found the mad venture progressing from wild risk and desperate defiance to daring demonstration, until he had solved the terrible puzzle of power and signs and criticism and opposition by declaring his leader no longer a prophet but the promised Son of God. This was the countryman certain that the authorities and the educated were going to capitulate, that they were being utterly discredited within their own stronghold, and then an hour later having to see his Messiah suddenly seized, mocked, condemned, crucified and not a finger raised to save him.

What had happened under such a strain? I could not say. I dared not say that the Eternal had not comforted this His child, had not saved him from despair and insanity. Nor would I say that the same God and Father of us all had forsaken His other child, who had trusted Him even more deeply, to suffer in utter discredit, despair and failure. The cry of the Psalms came again into my mind, "Thou wilt not leave my soul in the grave." What if God had answered his cry? The thought which had been forming in my mind as I wrestled with the tragedy and would help Saul in his agony also, recurred with fresh emphasis: what if, because Joshua had been both rash and also loving, trustful but also presumptuous, confident but yet daring to tempt the Most High and demand, as with an ultimatum, a vindication here and now, what if the Eternal had permitted him to suffer, and then given sign and proof that death is the gate of life? What if He had given His sign that His brave but impatient child was now declared an acknowledged son in what he taught, a chastened child in what he strove to fulfill in his own way and by his own will? If that hypothesis were correct, then would it not also explain this present situation? Was there not here before me the same case but a different example? This Galilean's Master had without doubt been his Master in every respect. The leader had used a slight degree of violence in his attempt to purge the House of God of a dubious traffic. The follower was already boasting of having called down death on two supporters who had tried to gain credit for giving more help than they actually had given. If this little group of believers were to continue to grow in character as their present leader had developed, then surely the love and humility I had heard preached in Galilee, and which I had welcomed as my own grandfather's teaching, would soon cease to be their possession. Certainly, defiance rather than meekness was growing in the man. Certainly, killing his leader had left the guidance of the group in far less creative hands.

But if we punished these men with long imprisonment, would they soften? If we killed them would not a still harder type take their place? My thoughts had led me on, so that reaching a conclusion in this question, I suddenly realized I was being asked another. The court was looking toward me, and, as it was clear I had not heard what had been said, the High Priest repeated:

"You are lately come amongst us appointed as a lawyer in Israel, a guide to judges, an interpreter of the Eternal Principles. Those of the Law who follow Shammai hold, as do we, that these men are blasphemous and working treason against the People. But you interpreters are divided. Now that the stern have spoken, let these rebels know they shall have justice, for the Merciful School of Hillel shall be heard." His voice was toned with a certain contempt. For the Levites and all the Sadducees are not displeased that the two great Schools of the Law, Shammai's and my grandfather's, should often be at variance. They feared lest, should the spirit of the synagogue and the Holy Scriptures speak with an undivided voice, much of their worldly practice and gain would stand condemned and that they must purge their house or find many forsaking their services.

For this reason I told the council what was on my heart. They attended closely as I pointed out that Theudas and Judas, who was also a Galilean, made risings. They depended solely on arms and preached no religion save revolt —their causes came to nothing. True religion had only to wait and God by other instruments than ours judged men and evil men perished. And now today were men before us whose only offense or defense so far was a rash loyalty to a convicted leader and their claim to perform miracles of healing in his name. (For the death of the fraudulent supporter and his wife I had no evidence to urge before a court, hearing of it only as a rumor and considering it only as an earnest of a spirit which if bullied would become brutal.) The prisoners' case, however, could and should be decided by argument, their claim to powers should be studied, their contention that their powers came from the dead should be subjected to scrutiny. Did not our sons often become healers and exorcists? Had there not been saints of the Temple and the synagogue of whom such stories had been told and credited? But, on the other hand, was it not known of my own grandfather Hillel the Holy that when the wise were gathered in council at Jericho the very *Bath Kol*, the audible voice of the Most High, was heard saying, "On one here would the Spirit have rested, if his generation had been worthy," and all knew that it was of Hillel the voice spoke, though he never performed a miracle.

At these words the elder Galilean interrupted. "But this day is the day spoken of by Joel the prophet: hence our miracles, our works, our signs."

I checked him by saying his own master had deprecated miracles and repeatedly denied us a sign. The court was impressed by this mild but effective way of checking his interruption and motioned me to continue. I came quickly to my conclusion. "Fathers," I said, "is it not clear that such movements as this, if they are left, will show whether they have in them the real spirituality they claim? If they have not, they will fail and many who misguidedly have gone into them will return to the fold won back by the patience of true shepherds. On the other hand, we know it is only by God's spirit that any spirituality can endure, and so if we attack these men indiscriminately we shall, if there be good in them, only be opposing God himself. My grandfather taught"—I saw Shammai's descendants shrug with contempt—"that the Most High is so merciful with us that we, if we would deserve His mercy, should be as merciful with those who offend us: He taught also that as the Eternal is a God of Peace we should always and to the utmost use peaceful methods with those we would convert. When tares have spread among wheat would you get rid of the weeds by burning the whole field? Must you not let both grow to the harvest? Then save the wheat and burn the weeds."

A few agreed with me; most were willing to wait and see how things would develop. They were suspicious of Caiaphas' violent ways and Annas' readiness to yield to him. Their antagonism came to a head three Passovers later when the High Priest's enemies persuaded the Roman governor Vitellius suddenly to depose this choleric ruler of Israel. Partly their hearts were touched, but in the main their motive was to thwart a man already impatient of the council's rights. With my support as a master of the Law they rallied and refused to entertain any capital charge. We of the Law, however, having given our rulings, withdrew and the executive council was left to decide how to deal with this difficult question.

My presentiment that any removal by death of the present leaders of the new movement would only uncover leadership more rash, was proved correct in the next few weeks. The new organization grew so quickly that the leaders were forced to create a relief service to look after the distribution of food. There were seven such secretaries to deal specifically with the commissariat questions. However, as might have been expected, one of these secretaries, instead of attending to his duties, began disputing with other Israelites who were far from willing to accept his dogmatic views. No doubt the movement was growing but it was in no sense a mass movement and part of my forecast was already confirmed. For every Jew who joined the group, another was repelled and incited to attack. The movement divided men passionately. Dramatic in its beginnings and instinct with elements of idealism and intolerance it was a ferment and never a cement. Most of those who joined were looking for an apocalypse. The preachers now openly said that their executed master, whose death they never denied but asserted, had not only been seen by them time and again but that shortly before they started on their campaign they had seen him float up from among them into the sky and that angels had informed them he was going to reappear shortly in the same manner. Others were attached to a movement of healing. Having recovered their health they stuck close to the source. Still others were ready to swell ranks where duties were not onerous and maintenance was provided free of charge. Naturally a group so provisional and heterogeneous would sooner or later invite attack. As I had said, the council could and should wait. Indeed the Roman power need not and probably would not intervene. The people of Israel themselves would decide whether the movement developing among them was a truer spiritual body than Temple or synagogue: whether this new teaching was a more apposite and fruitful interpretation of the Law and the prophets than that being given by the comments and applications made by us the scribes.

As a matter of fact, I heard nothing of this next crisis till it was all over. I was in my chambers when I heard Joab ask if I were free to receive visitors and at that moment Saul entered. I had never seen him so excited. His eyes were bloodshot. Sweat had dampened the hair on his forehead. I sat waiting for his salutation. He seemed almost unaware of me. Then after a perfunctory bow he broke out.

"We have been utterly mistaken. A fatal leniency! You, Master, are as responsible as anyone."

I told him that speaking when one was unprepared was always far worse than the greatest hesitancy. He drew his breath several times sharply through his nostrils. Then he began again more coherently but not more calmly.

"It all springs from that blasphemous Galilean."

"Well, your wishes were met: he is dead."

"You might well think he wasn't dead from the way the city is behaving."

"There is no rival like the dead," I quoted to him.

He turned on me what I first thought was a look of hatred but then I saw was fear—almost panic. However, he made another effort and went on:

"It's no use, though, if you cut down the tree but leave the suckers." Then with close on insolence, "You let those new leaders go. Had you permitted the council to strike then we should have had no more trouble, no more blasphemy."

"But if these men are less worthy than their leader, if they lack his charity and spirit and power, why think if they were removed that still more intemperate men would not take their place?"

"They *have*," he broke in. "But the heart of the People is sound if they are given proper support. There was no need to wait for official sanction, for court and council debate and summing up. It's all over."

"What?" I asked.

His tone was minatory. "As you have foretold, one of the hangers-on began picking quarrels with pious groups. They would not stand it. A Jew's religion is not to be played with, thank God. They took the fellow, after all patience was exhausted, and brought him along to a small vigilance committee which some of us younger devotees of the Law have formed. We feel that if our Elders won't give the sheep of Israel protection from wolves within the fold, we must. God shall not be mocked and we keep silent. We cross-questioned him, asking if he had said the blasphemous things they charged him with, the very things the late deceiver was accused of boasting—the Holy Temple's destruction and the abolition of the Law. And here is proof that madness had seized this base sect. The fellow, instead of answering, launched into a denunciation of us, the council, the Law. His face was like a madman's while he stormed and accused us. Naturally, after a while when he would not be silent, the crowd rushed to the bench we had set him on. We dragged him out of the Temple, denounced him as a blasphemer. Again he defied us. I told him to repent or there could only be one consequence. Again he defied us and the Law. The young men thereupon took stones and the penalty of blasphemy was paid. It was quick justice but justice, and necessary justice, it was. I stood by and saw it done. I do not shrink from saving holy things from profanation. Doing so will save many lives. Already the People are turning back to us. A vast crowd applauded the verdict. Already the sect is gone into hiding but I will hunt them out." His voice grew strident, "Don't you see: the time has come to strike. This is the time. Joshua the Galilean was simply a usurper. He did not deny the Law. All he wanted was to be acknowledged and crowned as the new Lawgiver, one greater than Moses. That merited death and what he earned he has paid. The second leader, Simon is his name, he's a vacillating fool, a temporizer, a hedger only brave when the dogs run from him. Then he'll pelt them, when, if they turn again he flees. He'll always be a wobbler. We can leave him alone. He's had one small beating. Mark my words you'll never see him again making trouble here. He may skulk back if it's safe. But at a wave of the lash he'll scuttle off, I'll wager, as far as Rome itself and hide himself in its vast slums and there bully simpletons. A single scowl and he'd cringe. Why, I'd join his own order of the scum, I'd join as an outsider and I'd beat him out of office if they would let me in for a fortnight. I'd make him take orders from me and when my back turned he'd try and betray his promise. I'd come back and he'd eat his words!"

The tirade was so violent that I rose and lifting my hand said, "Have you more to tell?"

"Yes, and then I'll be gone about my work. We struck at this Stephen because he was really dangerous. He had courage and a ready tongue. But the worst part of it is that he and his seven aren't Jews at all. Of course the Galileans aren't. But they would give anything to be Jews. Their one ambition is to have a prophet of their own recognized as a true prophet by us. A prophet out of Galilee, what ignorant nonsense, what impertinence! The Scriptures prove it, out of Galilee a prophet just cannot arise. Stephen was trying to bore from within and let a flood of polluting heathenism into the pure, revealed and solely true religion. But we've broken the spine of that rat and the rest of the swarm are on the run. Jerusalem, when we've gone through with it, will be clean again!" He paused, panting.

"Why," I asked, "have you come to tell me this?"

"Because you are so largely responsible for all this trouble. Your grandfather's school welcomed Greek thought and did not denounce it and always worked to loosen the binding of the Law. Hillel though Holy taught dangerous things. All men are not under the Fatherly protection of the Most High unless He has forgiven them their sin. This is only possible under the Covenant and by the blood sacrifice. And now what have we! The Law is loosened but the need in men's hearts, the sense of their guilt, is not met. Do you realize what these blasphemously Hellenizing Jews have been saying? Joshua said he was the Son of God but these men, may He forgive me, say that Joshua is the Most High. The seed of blasphemy has sprouted. It was inevitable. Men denied the true sacrifice and, knowing that blood must be shed, now say this deceiver's blood has redeemed them from the Law. It is ingenious, inevitable, diabolic."

"The Psalmist says, 'Ye are God's,' and it is also written, 'Sacrifice and oblation Thou wouldest not: then said I, 'Lo, I come, in the volume of the book it is written that I should do Thy will, O God.' "

He paused at my words. He looked so shaken and wretched that my heart went out to him, my tortured spiritual son. "Sit down my child." He obeyed. I put my hand on his shoulder. "My son, these are years in which the Most High tries us as silver is tried. We are taught to seek Him where new light is mixed with darkness and to see how darkened the old lamps are with age. The old clear distinctions are no longer evident. We of the Law are required to make plain what has become obscure and to find in the new and crude the old, the Eternal Truth. Joshua of Nazareth may have meant only to assert the truth the Psalmist promulgated that the Most High put His very spirit into man when He breathed into his nostrils the Breath of Life. And as to sacrifice, is not his life a true sacrifice for his faith and for his followers? May they not mean this very thing when they call him their Deliverer?"

For a moment I thought he would relax. But under my hand I felt the muscles of his shoulders tauten. He rose and almost flinging off my arm, "No! No! These are deadly pleadings. There can be no wavering, selecting, temporizing: finding good in evil and evil in good. They acclaim him a Saviour God, a Greek abomination yet ridiculous to the Greeks, for a God who was hanged can be no God to a

Greek. They say they must be saved and they are deadly right. They say the Law and its sacrifices cannot save them—they are deadly wrong. They say their man-God can save them—they are blasphemously wrong. They shall all die for it. The Law and its demands shall be maintained."

He ran from the room and I saw him no more. But two days later in the Temple court Zadok asked me if I approved my pupil's new charge. "The executive council," he replied to my question, "was importuned by him. He insisted this group of ignorant and superstitious Galileans was a real danger to the Law and the Temple and the reverences due to God Himself. He persuaded the council to grant him warrants to hunt the whole lot out of Jerusalem."

Joab, my servant, gave me my next information. "These Nazarenes are all gone, Sir. It looks as though strong measures do serve."

"Has even the fisherman Simon gone?" I asked.

"Yes Sir, I inquired particularly for I thought he was the head and very bold in his assertions. But he has fled north."

"Are none left?"

"There are a few devout and law-abiding souls who, I believe, hold the executed man to have been a prophet and they worship quietly in the Temple every day. But you could hardly hold them as of the new movement."

"The tragic episode is over then?"

"Your late student I judge, Sir, thinks not."

"How do you know?"

"The doorkeeper of the council chambers who is my friend, told me that today he reported to the Chief Priest that he had cleared the city, but that many malcontents had fled north, especially to Damascus. So he pressed for letters of authority that he might go there and finish off the business so thoroughly begun here. The Chief Priest gave him written authorization and he left the city for the north an hour after."

I dismissed Joab and sat thinking. The frantic zeal disturbed me. If the new sect were as deadly as he thought, was he not acting like an ignorant farmer who strikes at the stems of weeds and so scatters their seeds over his fields? Weeks passed and he never came to my chambers. Then one day at my door stood Caiaphas himself. He was more restrained with me since I was now of the Sanhedrin and my judgment had by law to be sought. But that he should come to my chambers showed he was in a difficulty he found it hard to confess. And his behavior confirmed my suspicion. I bade him be seated and would then have seated myself. He, however, begged me to sit down but himself walked over and looked out of that window, which gave on the wide area before the main gates of the Temple. I suddenly recalled it was here that Saul and I had looked down on Joshua's fateful essay to enter the Temple in triumph. Then without turning he asked,

"Have you had news of your pupil Saul?"

I told him, No, but that I had more reason to ask the question of him. "You sent him north. What has befallen him? He was my most rash, most promising, least settled student. Why did you send him on business which, if done at all, should be done by a tough man of arms?" I spoke insistently for I was moved, and expected Caiaphas to answer back as strongly.

But he did not. He paused and then said, "He forced us. He was so sure the matter must and could be closed. He had succeeded here. The issue was so grave. I said at the first trial that one man must die or the People be massacred by the Romans. If we did not rid ourselves of the false Messiah they would say we were supporting him and Pilate would slaughter us all. But later the issue was even graver.

If the new heresy grew, not only we and our families might be put to the sword, the very Law itself, the whole ritual of the Temple would be abolished and cast away. Saul asked to finish in Damascus what had been blessed with success here, to pursue the remnants rooted out in Jerusalem and to leave the land and the borders, those here and those abroad, free and clean of this contagion." He paused.

"Has he done it?" I asked.

His reply was a question, "Where is he?"

"I know nothing," I assured him.

Then the tall hard man bent and sat down, his head sinking between his shoulders. "All goes against me. I am a hated man. The council thwarts me and wants, I believe, even to degrade me from my office. The Most High is my witness I have served all my days the Holy Place, the altars and the Law. When you the wise doubted me and the ambitious and crafty coveted my power, in this young man burning with conviction and zeal, I put my trust." He paused. Then he went on with a voice that sank as his frame bent lower. "I could not believe it, were there anything else to believe. I came then to you believing, with a last hope, that you would be able to deny."

"Is he dead?" I asked with a sudden failing of the heart.

"I would to God he were: when I tell you, you too will ask the Most High to take away that life."

"In that Holy Name," I said, "tell me what has befallen my son you have misled."

He did not rebut my accusation but in a low voice repeated, "Had I received it from one or even two I could not have accepted it. Reason would not endure it. But after I heard, I made sure not once but again and always the story was the same."

"Tell me," I summoned him, standing before his bent form.

Almost in a whisper he said, "It is a poison, it is diabolic possession. Or are we, as you said, fighting against God who wills to destroy this place and us! Saul fell, as he was entering Damascus, fell as though struck by God. As he lay he spoke to someone unseen who, he believed, had smitten him. The smiter, he declared, he would now obey and that smiter he called—Joshua of Nazareth! Saul has vanished. He has been spirited away by these creatures we thought of as vermin. I traced him into Damascus. The company he took with him had among them some of my own servants. They lifted him up after his seizure and led him, for he appeared totally blind, into the city. There he lay helpless. One of them watched by him in the room which they had hired; while some started back for fresh orders, should he not recover. Several others consulted with the heads of synagogues in the city, delivering to them the letters which I had sent at Saul's request. One day when the watcher was alone, listening to Saul's delirium, for he was continually speaking to someone who was not there, the frightened attendant heard a step at the door. In came a poor creature whom he thought had blundered, while begging through the public rooms of the guesthouse. He says that he did not order the fellow out because he was glad of any company to relieve for a moment his vigil with a madman. But the fellow paid no attention to him, walked past him, went up to the bed on which the helpless Saul lay in delirium and called out loudly, 'Brother Saul! You may now see again!' My servant has reported on oath that, instantly, Saul leapt up, the beggar took him by the hand, and, as though they were lifelong friends, they walked straight past him, down the stairs and out into the street.

"From that moment until this, no one has seen Saul or indeed his abductor. There's not even been a rumor of them, inquire as we would. Damascus is filled with every false faith in the world. It is weeks now. He is lost. Perhaps they have killed him—I hear they claim to be able to kill by sorcery those whom they get into their power. Perhaps they hold him a blind captive in the desert. Perhaps they have bewitched him so that he has forgotten who he was and wanders himself a beggar."

Caiaphas paused. His voice had died away. His head was so sunken, I could not see his face. After a while he raised his eyes slowly till they met mine. In a voice flat with hopelessness he began again. "This is the loss of our spear-head. No one else had zeal. I, you do not need be told, am ringed with enemies of my own party, only desiring my fall that they may take my place. I would give the signet on my finger to know what has befallen him, even were the news the worst. Cannot you help me? Cannot you, at the least, suggest what may have happened?"

I held his eyes, looking up into mine, for several moments before I spoke. Then I said slowly, "In the list of possibilities which you have now given me you have left out one. Do you see what that one is?" I saw in his eyes a shadow of the same fear which I had so often seen lurking in the depths of Saul's. That fear overspread his whole face as I added, "The one possibility which you have yet to mention is that he may have become a follower of the very man. . . ."

"Of Joshua the deceiver!" It was almost a cry of panic.

"Caiaphas, you killed a man who was impatient to make to come at once that Kingdom of the Most High which we all are bound to pray may come. You drove him to his death and sent him to a horrible execution, executing upon him what was so largely your guilt and ours." He was silent and I went on. "I heard what Joshua taught in Galilee. It was the eternal good news of the love of God, our Father. That we should love Him as wholly as He loves us and that we should show forth that love by loving all our brothers, His children, as He has loved us—that was his gospel, that was his prophetic message. No one, priest, scribe or prophet but knows that this is the supreme word of God to Man. I saw that teaching harshen and lose the full embrace of its charity as it met the resistance of the timid and the conventional. When he came here, his patience, his bright sense of God's provision and unwearying purpose to work on every man only by love, that faith was giving out. Then your party struck, believing that by one act of violence you would save further bloodshed. With Joshua you might have treated. With his successor, Simon, you had a man of no vision but with a certain loyalty to his master and a certain uncreative simplicity in retailing his master's message. He had lived with Joshua and heard his teaching. Unfertile and superstitious as he was, he would not distort his teacher's words, though he might worship his master as Messiah himself. Simon, too, you might have conciliated and kept within the fold had your wish been solely to shepherd the Holy People and to keep the flock of the Lord undivided. But Saul, I know as few can know him. I know that he never knew, never spoke one word with Joshua. When he saw him he was filled with passionate resentment, such a resentment that I could not fail to realize how some deep conflict in his nature was roused to frenzy by the problem of Joshua's nature. Believe me, Saul will not and cannot care for that Eternal Gospel which Joshua taught and which to me and to all of my grandfather's School is so lovely, so healing and so authentically inspired. His concept of the Most High, as Our Father, is clouded by a sense of guilt and a terrible need to find appeasement. He sees the Eternal in his own image. He fought Joshua and his followers because he sees, and they see, in the prophet of Galilee, not one who told them of a Father who forgives if they forgive, but a mysterious sacrifice who can carry away the guilt of their sin. Saul hated Joshua because he could not be quite certain whether this, his supreme need, could be met. He needed forgiveness, and yet he feared to expose his need. Now he is gone over to that allegiance because now he has convinced himself, not that Joshua is a prophet whose message may be confirmed by the prophets and which fulfills the Law and is acknowledged in our hearts; but because the man of Nazareth is now his Saviour God."

At those words Caiaphas threw back his head. "Then," he said, "you are right. Joshua threatened the People's peace and their earthly lives but this Saul using Joshua's name will batter, sap and undermine the Law itself. He will, if he succeeds, destroy our holy and only true religion. I would prefer that not one stone stood upon another in this sacred place rather than that this mighty building might remain and the Law be banished and this house of the Most High remain only like the abandoned temple of a God whose faith has vanished. I would, before Heaven, that I had spared your prophet. Why did not I try to understand him? I thought I was stamping out a spark in the granary. I have thrown a lighted brand into the ripe harvests of the world."

He rose and left me without another word. Being High Priest he prophesied truly. Had we shown deep charity toward the last of the prophets sent us by the Most High, had we cherished real humility toward our fellow men, had we kept this man within the fold, then we might have learned from him and he from us, and authority itself would have been strengthened. For me, too, there would have been the added comfort that we should not have driven beyond our reach, that powerful but untamed son of my school and of my teaching with his strange variant of the Law of Love.

Chapter X

SO, *I THOUGHT*, the story was ended. But we creatures of Time have not the patience of the Eternal. His thoughts are not our thoughts nor His ways our ways. I was still to see this mysterious history I was imagining as closed and over, develop even more strangely than it had begun.

The years were passing. Caiaphas was gone. Another of the house of Annas, a puppet of the Romans, was in his place. I knew that the movement, whose source I have disclosed, was still in progress. The followers of Joshua had first been known as Nazarenes. When, however, their organization spread as far as the Greek cities of the north, they came to be called Christians, the Greek word for Messianists. Indeed the sect was beginning to be almost as widely spread as the Dispersion itself.

But those who would observe the Law still found their natural home in the Temple. Let such as would charge us of Israel with the spirit of vindictive intolerance remember this. Any who would revere Joshua as a true prophet and indeed as the spiritual Messiah, the perfect fulfiller of the Law, the one who was sent to teach that love gives us the power so to fulfill it, they were accepted and respected in the Temple. Indeed it was a brother of Joshua, one Jacob, the man who had been mentioned in the old Nazareth scribe's description of the early days of that fateful mission, who now led the little flock. He was a simple man deeply practised in prayer and so enduring at it that they said of him that his very knees had become calloused like a camel's. What I know is that those who seek the Most High will of His mercy obtain hearts of great tenderness and souls most lowly. This Jacob had led those souls who sought to follow Joshua's teaching and had been left without a leader when the original leaders all had fled.

One day as I was passing through the courts by the spot where he generally prayed, I stopped. My eye was held by the simple peace that held his upturned face as in the calm of a waiting child. It was late in the afternoon, the colonnade deserted. Yet, according to his custom, he was continuing in prayer. Here, then, I reflected, is another fruit of a prophet's teaching. Saul has by that impact, by his utter refusal to accept the message in its true sense, been thrown headlong into the midst of those very Gentiles whom he had despised, and all his ties with the Law have been broken. Simon, the bewildered companion of Joshua, was still in a vertigo from that contact and still wavering as to what that message could mean and how that gospel could be lived. And here was Jacob, Joshua's own brother, closer to him than Simon, Jacob, the elder brother, who had known the brilliant child, watched his growth, been troubled by his beginnings, deeply distressed by his final steps and then patiently submissive to the tragic earthly end. Jacob, with far more intimate understanding than Simon or Saul, and with far slower reaction than either, Jacob, at last had made up his mind. Turning over all the story in his simple but brave understanding, slowly weighing its entire significance with his just conscience, he had come to his conclusion.

Humbly he accepted the fact that in the younger brother whom he had tried to protect and had failed either to influence or to understand, God had visited his People. Accepting this, with all the mystery of evident suffering, apparent failure and the final enigmatic signal from beyond the tomb, Jacob waited here for God by further Word to show the further way. And, as I knew, many simple and just people were of his mind and waited with him. Their belief lay, I think, in this—that as God had begun to speak He would, if they kept silence, complete the message, the first words of which came through brother Joshua, now their elder brother, the first born of the new dispensation. They would not rush out and complete through their own efforts, and against their own People, the Most High's new utterance of warning and invitation.

These thoughts were in my mind as I looked on that calm face. Through the light that flashed through Joshua, the mask of arrogant contempt which Saul had worn was stripped from him, revealing underneath the raw working features of the tortured soul desperately seeking safety. That same light melted from the face of Simon the callouses of routine self-assurance, another mask built up by years of canny success at his hard-won craft. Beneath that mask was exposed a face swept by indecisions, snatching at assurance, at leadership, at domination, and as quickly seeking to placate and hastening to surrender. And here was a third countenance exposed, illuminated, revealed in and through that light. Here to prejudiced scribe and impulsive fisherman was added the patient carpenter. "Each trade only understands its trade"—the journeyman's maxim came into my mind. Perhaps this Jacob, the brother and fellow craftsman of Joshua, really understood him best; had learned most from him, had grasped the idea of the yoke which Joshua had desired to fashion and had begun patiently to carry it.

Certainly the man whose face I watched while it remained calmly unaware of me, had seen a light and that light was leading him into the path of peace. Indeed, as he prayed there silently, I became aware through his patient waiting that here in the outer court I was present at audience granted by the Most High. At the sense of that Presence I bowed as Moses in the wilderness before the burning bush. I cannot say how long we remained. I found Jacob standing beside me in an attitude wherein were blended courteous respect and gentle independence. We spoke without any awkwardness of restraint.

"God declares His will to us in many ways," he began. It was a simple opening but I understood his mind and what he wished to say.

"Yes, this the Temple, the Holy Law and the Voice of the Most High speaking in the depth of the silent heart, these are His three Voices to us."

"So I have found it," he replied with a grave equality, "in this Holy Place it is good to pray. The air is of the Eternal and the heart opens to the heavens while the Law and the prophets teach us how to pray." Then becoming more particular, "Do not think that we who have found him of whom the prophets speak despise Law and Temple. God forbid. Did not he himself whom God has sent, tell us that every detail of the Law shall be fulfilled? He has given us new power in our hearts to observe in spirit as well as in deed what till then was little more than an obligation. To those of us who feared our Father, because we felt that we could never really fulfill His Laws, He has shown that by love the Law is fulfilled, that perfect love casts out all fear. A child who loves his Father cannot fear the One who has taught him to love. And," turning to me with a quiet obeisance, "he added particularly that as you sit in Moses' seat we should attend to all your counsel."

"We wish," I encouraged him, "only to keep the Law and to make it observable in spirit and in truth."

"I believe you," he said gently and then after a pause, "may I speak with you of our new hope, our new faith in what the Law is meant to tell us?" We had fallen into a slow walk side by side. As we paced the wide cloisters, empty and cool, the good man gave me his confidence. "Sometimes I fear, Master, that others may have given you a mistaken view of what we the closest followers of our Master practice, preach and believe."

"Often I have wished, friend," I replied, "that I might speak with those of you who love the Law."

We spoke until the great court was already in dusk and the last rays of the sun were slanting up until they could only be touched by the Temple's tallest pinnacle, a point of gold against the deepening blue. I led him to the gate to pass him through the guards, but they evidently knew him well enough. We went up the inner steps on which I had stood that last time I was with Joshua. Hc paused. "Master, you see we plan no schism. We are full unalienated children of Abraham, followers of Moses."

"Yes," I said, "as my devotion to holy Hillel makes me not less but more a zealous servant of the Law, so you following Joshua are also, as God has shown you, fulfilling the Law. We are surely one as notes of a chord are one."

He was silent. I could see he was satisfied, but he wanted still to ask me something further. Then as the postern door was being opened for him, his request came: "There are some younger scribes with us. They find us devout and observant, if ignorant. They have asked several times wise elder men to sit with us to give counsel when we who are simple have to decide on our actions as a group. Next week an issue confronts us which will tax our simplicity." He paused. "Others are coming to be with us—others who now have been far away for some time. One who was greatly learned in the Law and who yet has departed, as it seems to me, greatly from it, is coming to us." He paused again.

My heart warmed by charity and by the especial love

which a father feels at news of a prodigal, suddenly gave me light. "My child Saul?" I questioned.

"Yes, yes, it is he." Then as the porters waved Jacob toward the unbarred door, as he bowed to me he asked, "May I come tomorrow and seek your counsel?"

"Go in God's peace," I blessed him, "and come tomorrow most gladly." We raised our right arms in blessing and the postern shut behind him.

I detected a pleased surprise on Joab's face as he came and stood before me the following afternoon. In my house an upright servant is even as a son, he gives filial devotion and is given paternal care in return. I answered, "Say on," to his request, "Master, may your servant speak before you?" and Joab began, "I myself often thought that a Galilean could be little good. But there is a holy man who has won many by his humble sanctity. Indeed some of my friends, very devout people, worship with him and his group. They have gained such peace in their hearts from his teaching and by prayer with him that they no longer find themselves troubled with such issues as when and how shall Messiah come and should they or should they not join the Zealots. . . . "

"I know," I interrupted him, and smiling at him, "do not keep the good man waiting longer. Bring him up."

Smiling back at me at the discovery that his gentle diplomacy had not been needed, Joab withdrew, reappearing in a few moments with Jacob. We saluted each other in the Holy Name. On my asking him to seat himself beside me I could not but notice the humble dignity with which he accepted. "Surely," I reflected, "long waiting in the Presence of the Eternal gives any soul such a sense of its own insignificance that human disparities cease to embarrass it. With the same unhurried quiet, he spoke immediately to the heart of his problem.

"Sir, to your judgment, I am told, we owe our liberty. And not ours only but the liberty of those others of us who—we of Jerusalem believe—may be moving toward license.

"True, the Sanhedrin listened to my plea that only the life lived can of certainty establish or disprove the doctrine. We know, of a surety, through the mercy of the Father's Covenant with us, the path through which we may come to holiness if we will. But we also know that His Mercy is wider than our judgment and he may draw others through ways strange to us, hidden and dark. Of these others we may only be sure when their ways and that way vouchsafed to us converge and meet at the Throne of the Father."

"It is because you, a master in Israel, a voice of the Law, has so spoken, that we can but turn to you. In you, we know, the Justice of the Law and the Mercy of the All Merciful have met. Here then is our issue. Simon, whom your voice spared and Saul whom your charity reared, now claim to be the authoritative voices of our teaching."

I could not resist a father's affection urging me to ask, "What of Saul? Is he at peace?"

"I myself," Jacob answered quietly, "find it easier to answer that question than others. But may I first tell you of Simon? Simon is one of my kind. All my life I have known him. When I have told you of him, may we together speak of that one, known well to you, above me in the Law, beyond me now that he goes beyond the Law. When the persecution that Saul set on foot drove out those disloyal to the Temple, Simon fled north. It was, surely, unsafe for any of us to remain. We who stayed, stayed on because we believed that our simple witness to the teaching of love to all and obedience to authority, as long as authority spoke in the spirit of the Law, was required of us. You had extended to us the hope of protection. Should we therefore fail to answer your call by an equal trust? That was my counsel. As you know, the other Jacob, who was one of my brother's first followers, was killed. Herod beheaded him on a charge of treason. When I was called on to lead our group here, I felt it was our duty to establish an innocency by showing we have no political aims. Joshua's teaching, I hold, was that his followers should fulfill completely the Law of spiritual righteousness. But those who fled began to teach beyond the Holy Land. They have said things which may well appeal to the Gentiles, because they are attacks, untrue attacks, upon us the Jews. They say often now, I hear, that nearly all the rulers and most of the People rejected Joshua's teaching. That, we know, is not true."

I bowed. He paused and then went on, almost to himself, "Simon is a good man. He loved Joshua, though he was not Joshua's best friend. Indeed I often think that had I, his brother, been more humble and understanding, had I been able to realize. . . . " Then turning to me, "Rabbi, you who have cared for us of the outskirts, you will realize how hard it was for us to understand that God visited us. It seemed presumptuous that to our lowly door, out of our family, banished so far from the royal city of Bethlehem, should come the Lord's messenger. We hung back, we who might, who should have helped. Naturally more impetuous souls pushed forward."

Again he was silent and then added slowly, "I know Simon bar Jonah has never been certain what Joshua meant. He thought that he, the simple fisherman, was to sit with his fellows on thrones judging the Tribes and that to him in particular was granted a primacy and a unique authority over men's souls. How could such a one fail to urge Joshua to take the Messianic Kingdom? He has boasted in my hearing that it was he who made Joshua certain that he must go up to Jerusalem and claim the throne."

"And then he failed his master," I added.

"It was then," continued Jacob, "that I began to see light. Up to that time, Joshua's message had been an increasing mystery, and indeed a bitter problem to me. But once Simon had had his way, and the way had," he paused, "had ended, ended by God's will showing that there was no road to an earthly kingdom—then God's mercy opened to our eyes the real, the really royal and divine road. I know," and he turned to me in the conviction of a simple, demonstrable faith, "I know Joshua lives and in the light of his risen eternal life I know at last what his gospel means." He was silent, his face irradiated with a peace and strength which I knew the world could never take away. Then he added quietly, "And I know that the way we are following here in fulfilling the Law is the way he would have us go. I dare add also that though Simon and he who was once your pupil may gain successes in and with the world, always will their doctrine be confused with the world which they would meet and win. If they would be free of the Law they will only find themselves caught in the webs of Gentile sophistries and cults. I will prove it. Already the tree bears fruits, as Joshua told us it would. Simon when here ruled sternly."

I bowed, to show that I knew.

"Should one forgiven have been so stern?" Jacob saw that I, too, dared not say Yes to that question. "Then," he continued, "Simon again fled and when safe in the north at Joppa had a vision which he held relieved him of our diet rules. This certainly would aid him by popularizing his doctrine with the Gentiles. But need we take such visions as revealing God's will for us to disregard the Law?"

Again my silence answered his question as his simple heart had answered it.

"Yet had my heart then failed me," his voice gained power and gentle authority, "my faithlessness would now have been rebuked. For now Simon wishes to come and take counsel with us here and your disciple comes also. I will tell you all I know," he added, for he saw the keenness of my desire. "He has been, I am told, preaching far further afield, far out among the Greeks. And the wider his doctrine has been spread, the further it has departed from the Law and the less has he mentioned the actual teaching of our Lord. And now they are coming home, home to ask our blessing and our judgment. They are asking have they not taught Joshua's message. I do not ask—for that would not be just—'Tell me what should we say?' What I ask is, 'Would you come among us and be present, so that when appeal to the Law is made, we, simple but unsubtle in our loyalty, may give reason for the faith that is in us?' "

He ceased, and I pondered. Could I refuse? My heart longed to see my son Saul again. I wished too to see the fisherman who first had told me of Joshua and later had by my pleading been let go out into the world which like tinder was waiting for a spark of any faith to set it ablaze.

"I will come," I said.

He rose, making his obeisance of departure and concluding, "I thank the Most High for his loving-kindness shown in you to the simple. May He reward."

The next week he called as he had arranged. With only Joab to accompany me, I went with him to the place where the Poor Men or Ebionites, as they were called, met. The house was in a poor quarter, but at the top overlooking the city it had a long roof chamber which was spacious and well lit.

Several groups had already arrived and had formed knots

which conversed together hardly noticing one another. Those who were nearest us as we entered seemed least at ease, staying hard by the door. Their accent betrayed them as much as their dress. So it was only a requirement of courtesy for Jacob to inform me: "These are scribes who like yourself have kindly come to act as consultants should we of the conservative party need help in stating our case for holding closely to the Law." We bowed to each other. They were younger Rabbis, and, of course, liberals—else they would not have ventured on such an errand of charity. I knew most of them by sight and some by name. Heartened by the arrival of an Elder, their assurance rapidly returned and they had just begun to question me as to how best they might help these inquirers, when we were interrupted. The group nearest ours was the most animated. While all the others conversed in low tones these seemed to be in the highest spirits. They had, indeed, just burst into laughter when out from their midst broke a small man. He, making straight for me, to the surprise of my fellow scribes, took me by the hand, shaking it vigorously. "Why, brothers," he almost shouted, "this is a great day. You know, when the master comes to learn from the pupil then we have still another sign that the New Age is here!"

The silence was not encouraging. In the silence I could feel their contempt mingled with the surprise I too was experiencing. The change in Simon, remarkable as it had been, was nothing compared to that wrought in Saul. Genial openness and boisterous elation were the last characteristics that his closest friend could ever have detected in Saul, the Pharisee. In the man before us, they eclipsed every other feature. My interest in seeing such a change did not prevent my noticing my junior colleagues' stiffening disapproval at one of their contemporaries—and one who had lost caste completely—treating as an equal an Elder of

Israel. Nor did my relief at Saul's obvious health, make me any the less anxious to discover the grounds for his apparent enthusiasm. I did not have to ask, however.

"Master," he burst out, catching me by the hands, "I now see (and I thank Him) why the Most High put me at your feet and in your train. You, with your teaching of the Law, you were the tutor to lead me to Messiah Joshua."

I saw my fellow hearers wince. One of them I judged to be on the point of an angry outburst. In order to preserve outward peace and lest we should break up before any good had been effected, I asked,

"Surely you would not deny that the Holy Law has brought those who observed it to righteousness and peace?"

His face twitched and I saw for a moment before me the tortured youth I had known. But in a flash the new visage reasserted itself.

"No man reverences the Law more than do I; I indeed reverence it more than any of you! I know that the Law is so high that no man may attain it. There!" he said with the quick outwardly intimate turn of the public speaker. "There, that was precisely where I was. The learned Master Rabbi here will answer for that. Won't you, Teacher!" And of course not waiting for the rhetorical question to be answered, he ran on.

"A Pharisee of the Pharisees, of the Tribe of Benjamin, at the feet of Gamaliel." He swept a practised gesture which both saluted me as an authority and also drew me in as testimony. "Oh, you may be sure with such ancestry, such breeding, such teaching and, I give you my word for it, with such a desperate will, why if the Law *could* have been fulfilled—I say it with utter humility—it *would* have been fulfilled. And I say with equal factual honesty—it was not! It stood, it stood like stone in my path and I stood, work as I would,"—his voice sank deep—"condemned! And then I suddenly saw in a flash. Aren't there two great elements in the Holy Covenant? The Law, yes, but also the Sacrifice. The Law had grown clearer and clearer and the Sacrifice less and less clear."

It was fine ad hominem arguing. I saw that his quick sense of his listeners' outlook had allowed him to capture the attention of his listeners in spite of their prejudices. My sense of his new power as a propagandist rose further when he added with a studied carelessness,

"Of course you see it all turns on the resurrection of the dead. The Sadducees, confined to the old idea of sacrifice and to the old ignorance as to what lies beyond death, cannot see this. But you Pharisees realize the problem as well as I do. You know there is a future life."

They agreed guardedly, but with growing interest.

"It's clear, then, isn't it, what kind of sacrifice God would and could only accept, and"—his audience began to shift uneasily—"how God would show, would *prove* that this was the only acceptable sacrifice. For our justification, to save us from the death penalty of the broken Law which we couldn't fulfill, He would sacrifice His son and He would raise him up again. Blood is needed. Without the shedding of blood, sin can't be discharged. The blood of cattle will not do. The argument is irresistible. The blood of God's son saves and that alone saves."

They did not answer; they simply drew aside. I heard one say, "What a fantasy: a Greek gloss on Hebrew truth." "If a man is a false prophet and is convicted and executed," said another, "what better proof would you ask that God has disowned him?" For a moment I saw a flash of bitter contempt pass over Saul's face. Then abruptly he turned his attention wholly to me:

"Master," and his face filled again with its former elation, "it is true, the Law is fulfilled."

"Our Father is as merciful as He is just," I replied, "I agree the Law can be fulfilled."

"No! No!" he expostulated. "Only Messiah can fulfill it and he has." I was silent and he broke out again. "How can you of all men doubt it? You can't have forgotten what I was, bound, frightened, full of dread and resentment. Look at me now!"

The change was indeed a revolution, a transmutation of character.

"Surely to you this must be the proof. See, I have received manifest forgiveness. I am a new creature. I have love, joy, peace. These are the sure marks of all of us who have received the Spirit of our risen Master. You can't explain it otherwise. I was not only a crabbed bitter creature. I tried to exterminate his Faith. It made no difference. Me, chief of sinners, he took. Through none of his apostles has he worked greater wonders—indeed none so great!"

"Is everyone yielding to your teaching in the outer countries?" I asked.

"All that are to be saved." His answer was shot with a tone of counterchallenge I could not disregard. He read my question before I spoke it. "Those who believe the doctrine are saved. They receive the Spirit. It comes on them with authenticating power. They heal and themselves become saviours. Those who refuse get nothing: they have rejected the Light. If, then, anyone dares to teach otherwise, I must and do condemn him. I have told all my converts that even if an angel from heaven should tell any one of them anything different from what I have said, he is damned. He is accursed!" The old Saul had returned. Dark and menacing came the words: "They are outside the plan of salvation. Only one way is offered by God to men whereby they may be saved. I know. It is the precious blood—it is Moses' teaching—and the precious lamb is the Messiah." He paused and his voice deepened still more: "It is true, some have resisted the salvation which Messiah Joshua, God's Sacrifice, confided to me to preach and I have cut them off. Those who blaspheme my gospel or preach it in any other way are poisoners of the only well of Life. I have already handed over more than one such to Satan that he may teach them."

I was seeking with prayer how to answer, if any answer there were. At my shoulder I heard a gentle voice. It was Jacob's.

"Friends, we are now ready to discuss. Will you be seated." Then aside to me, "The younger scribes, Rabbi, felt that their help would be of no avail. But if you will stay we shall have all the aid we desire or require."

Much as I would now have wished to retire, I felt it was my duty to remain. I asked, though, that I might be seated out in the gallery, so that, unless Jacob should specifically ask my judgment on some point of the Law, I might remain a silent and detached witness. Jacob consented and quickly collected the rest. It was then that I caught sight of Simon for the first time since his trial. And here, again, I could not but be struck by the same strange mingling of appearances, which I had perceived in Saul. It was as though two persons were inhabiting the one body and striving to express their conflicting characters in one face. In Saul the old fearful and resentful nature was shot through, but not dissipated, by a new peace and love. In Simon timidity and self-assertion alternated; sudden convictions of faith were striated with panic qualms of insecurity.

Jacob, with quiet assurance in which all seemed to assent, began by saying that their need to express their fundamental agreement had brought them together. For his part he felt a growing assurance that the Messiah was being revealed to them as prophesied by Moses, a Messiah who should fulfill the Law. "Brothers," he said, "may we not all thank our Father that through His son He has shown us how he who is the glory of the People of Israel is also the Light to lighten the Gentiles."

Saul stirred at this, his face lit with pleasure, his lips half parted to speak. Jacob, however, went gently on: "He told us that the whole Law should be fulfilled. We of the Law are charged, therefore, to fulfill it, to show that by his mandate and through his power the Law eternal can now be made actual."

"But he made us free of the Law," broke in Saul.

"No: free to fulfill the Law. In that service we find perfect freedom."

"Then you are going to bind the Gentiles!"

There was a pause. "Let us first make clear our own position," Jacob resumed. To this Simon seemed to give a species of assent and I saw Saul flash at him a look of anger. "We are Hebrews," went on Jacob, "but we must prove that the Law can be fulfilled."

"But it can't be, save by blood. Blood, yes, but inevitably human blood for human sin."

The shock that was obviously felt by Jacob and his friends at this dreadful statement seemed only to spur on Saul. "And it has been shed, offered, accepted." In his voice exultation and defiance, anger and delight were terribly mingled. "Messiah Joshua's blood, that and that alone redeems. It saves from sin: it sets us free, absolutely free. Faith, just faith in that, that's all!"

"But faith, if you do nothing, isn't alive. It can't be. The tree must have fruits?" Jacob questioned gently.

"Works! Works! Trying to fulfill the Law yourself! That's death! That's damnation! God will damn those who think, who dare think they can fulfill the Law necessary for life.

Only Messiah Joshua's death and his blood can save. The Gentiles are turning by multitudes and becoming part of the true Israel, the new Israel. Are we going to tie them up to the barren Law? Messiah Joshua made them free." Then turning to Simon, who had been looking from one to the other uneasily, "Simon!" he called in pre-emptory command. "Stand bravely for what you've done. You did eat with the saved Gentiles in the new Liberty. You've broken the Law. Have the courage to say so. Don't shilly-shally!"

"Well, well," Simon replied, "I did show, I hope, a proper friendliness, but . . . . "

"Oh, I know," cut in Saul, "when those"—and the look of scorn flashed for a moment to Jacob himself—"who say that the Gospel is simply the Law fulfilled and not the Law transcended, challenged you, you recanted. But remember, too, that when I, the humble instrument of the new revelation, confronted you with your lack of faith and candor you saw your fault. You are now clear and definite —are you not?"

The voice was so harsh that its hectoring tone suddenly awoke a memory. I recalled Saul, still a Pharisee, still a pillar of the purest Law, in a sudden outburst of contempt for this very Simon and his leadership, swearing that the man was so weak that he, Saul, if he chose to join the movement, could make such a leader his puppet. That railing attack, that bitter jest, meant to prove by its extravagance the weakness of the whole movement, had rebounded like a curse on its utterer's head. For though here he was proving that he could dominate Simon, it was at the price which he never imagined he would have to pay—a deeper submission than any Simon had had to make.

Jacob intervened. His gentle spirit saw how to save the situation. "Brethren, we should decide about the Gentiles. We Hebrews have our faith fulfilled in Joshua. What should those who have come first to him and then to the Law know of the Law? What of it should they keep?"

His voice as much as his actual words directed the meeting. Simon, who had been struggling to defend himself, gladly accepted the ruling which would save him from so fierce an antagonist as Saul. And Saul's keen mind, seeing a practical administrative problem being raised, left the pursuit of a foe he despised to take action where he could shape the future. Immediately his face was transformed. It became like an angel's, radiant, gentle, benign. The flame of self-giving love lit it up with a sudden glory. Jacob could embrace such a spirit as generously. Simon glowed with a generous relief in which all vindictiveness was burned away. The three and their companies were one, united in their desire to give the Gospel to the world.

"He is with us now," said Simon, and in the simplicity of that conviction they all bowed their heads in silence. I felt the Presence of the Peace of the Eternal and gladly bowed my head also. It was Simon again who gave expression to the thought of unity. "The Gentiles will surely keep the Law Eternal and Universal. As to those special aids and guides which God has given us, to help us fulfill the Two Great Commands, surely if they aid they should be kept but if they do not aid, then the Gentiles should be free?"

"Yes, I see they should be free in all dietary rules," Jacob contributed. "Still you would not expose them to the danger of idolatry by leaving them to purchase their food in those markets where it has already been offered to heathen idols?" Both Simon and Saul immediately agreed: the group was a unity of charity. Encouraged, Jacob added, "Brothers, one thing more. Our holy faith teaches that in blood some unknown mystery resides and so we are warned to abstain from it. May we not ask this, too, of the Gentiles, for their good?"

Again not only Simon but Saul agreed. Saul might have opposed this limit on the extreme freedom with which he wished to commend his faith to the wide world. But not only was the spirit of charity now so keen in the group that each clearly wished to share the other's desires, but his own doctrine had actually retained and emphasized the blood as necessary to fulfill the Law. With alacrity he, therefore, welcomed Jacob's plea. Simon I saw for a moment reflect. Jacob and Saul in close alliance—that alone would sway him. But as I watched him I saw assent open into increasing welcome. Some thought was spreading through his mind.

"Yes," he said, and then with growing animation, "yes, brothers, those are the two essentials. I see it now. We shall thrust the false gods of the heathen from their altars and we will offer a pure sacrifice instead."

"It is offered here at Jerusalem?" Jacob answered. There was a question in his voice. Simon did not seem to hear. Some vision appeared to be dawning within him. "Brothers," Jacob therefore resumed, "we are all agreed. I will stay here with the fold of Israel. You will go out among the Gentiles gathering in all who answer the call of our Master, that there may be one flock and one shepherd."

The whole company arose and Jacob, lifting his arms, gave them the blessing. A deep peace descended on the upper room. For a timeless moment one felt the Eternal Presence. Even when time again resumed its passage, I did not pass straight back into the Jerusalem of that day. Instead there was a strange transitional period. I had no vision, but surely my soul was passing through that area between the Eternal and the Current, that station from which the prophet beholds mankind and its story. This I know and this I shall not forget. I felt myself as a wanderer, crossing a high range of mountains when he comes to a spot where at his feet a small spring creeps from the rock to take its way toward the valley. As his eyes range further to follow its course he catches miles away glimpses of great rapids, then further again broad stretches of a wide river until finally across the blue distance of the plain he perceives an estuary deploying into the ocean itself.

I was roused by someone's speaking. The eye of the Spirit closed and I saw before me Saul—or should I not now call him Paul? So he was calling himself, claiming his Roman citizenship. And certainly in the face that confronted mine, it was not the forehead stripped of the sacred frontlets and the hair shorn like a Roman's, that assured me that I was gazing at a new man, one who no longer looked to Jerusalem and the past and to the Law, but to the future, to the freedom that he would carve for those who followed him. The question in my mind he answered.

"Well, Master, I go to the Gentiles. The Greek and the Roman will grasp what God has given Israel and what Israel still cannot submit to and accept!"

"I am going, too," another voice answered, and Simon was at his shoulder.

Jacob would have shepherded them down the outside staircase that led from the gallery. But Paul swung round on Simon: "There's no need. You can stay here. I know what the Gentiles need and can understand. They need salvation. I will set them free both from the Law and the Temple Sacrifices. I have seen it done. Just by the name of Messiah Joshua, just by knowing that he died for them and rose, nothing more is necessary. They are made new creatures. I will conquer the whole world with just that!"

He made a movement to push Simon back. Suddenly,

however, the small rugged fisherman became alive. He put wide his arms, pressing aside both Paul and Jacob.

"No! No!" And he spoke with authority which, because it was so sudden and unexpected, arrested all of us. "No!" he said a third time with rising emphasis. "Neither you, Jacob, far less you, Saul, declared him. It was I! He called me the Rock. I am the foundation, the threshold. You may be the posts on either side. I am the stone on which you stand, the threshold over which all men must pass into the Kingdom. He gave to me the power to open and to close—to me!"

He stopped and they waited on him. Then his eyes dilated and almost in a chant his voice recited, "Neither Jew nor Gentile but a New Temple and a New Sacrifice: Neither the Law nor the Sacrifice offered once, but an ever-repeated Sacrifice. Not a free salvation bought by merit, not a new creature wrought in a moment, not a sudden magical perfection of Sanctity. No! but sinners ever sinning and ever being forgiven. Absolution and grace granted ever and again. Such is the way. Nor will this be, as you, Jacob, would have it, a clinging to the past, here in Jerusalem. Jerusalem and this Temple, as he prophesied, shall perish. Nor as you, Saul, would make it, a licensed freedom in every wandering soul. No, there is a city where power and spirit meet, where a false priest calls himself Supreme Pontiff. Thither I go in the name of my Master. I am his Vicar. Thither I go to found the true priesthood of our Messiah. I am the first true Pontifex Maximus. I go to take Rome!"

We were all struck dumb. Paul first recovered: "You boast! You'll run away!"

"Maybe," flashed back the fisherman, "but I'll come back. He'll drag me back!"

"I'll go to Rome, too."

"You will have to teach what I teach."

"Very well, come, we will see which he will choose."

"To Rome!"

The cry came from them both. In this astounding venture they were agreed. The name spurred them. As their footsteps died away I heard once more their voices rise from the stairway in challenge and defiance as each urged the other to trial by ordeal, "To Rome!"

Jacob and I were alone. All the others had gone.

"Is this the end, Master?" he said turning to me.

"No!" It was now my turn to say No. "We serve the Eternal and we know that because He is the Eternal for those who trust in Him the end is ever but the beginning."

Such has been that beginning. Now the world knows another Faith. But this I still know: that whether through prophet or through priest, whether through Sacrifice and Temple or synagogue and sacred roll, the Eternal and His Law shall abide for ever.

www.ingramcontent.com/pod-product-compliance
Lightning Source LLC
La Vergne TN
LVHW050644100826
845148LV00011B/1968

* 9 7 8 1 6 0 6 0 8 9 8 2 8 *